Praise for *When Words*

"It doesn't take long to realize that leadership at any level in any organization is subject to criticism. That's why Warren Bullock's book *When Words Hurt* is a must read! It's biblically grounded and spiritually insightful! In this book, I felt like I was sharing a good latte with a great leader, gleaning practical wisdom from his public and private life! I will be giving this book to several of my friends!"

Doug Clay, secretary-treasurer, The General Council of the Assemblies of God

"In *When Words Hurt* Dr. Warren Bullock shares the keen insight of a decorated warrior coupled with the godly wisdom of a tender-hearted statesman discussing how to handle some of the most challenging aspects to ministry. The transparency and authentic style of Warren's writings provide a timeless teaching tool for anyone who wants to serve the Lord over the long haul in building God's kingdom. When you read this book, be prepared to hear Jesus' voice in dealing with those who are critical of your ministry."

Scott Erickson, lead pastor, Peoples Church, Salem, Oregon

"Warren Bullock is the ideal counselor for leaders. He is wise, experienced, biblically informed, and an excellent communicator. This new book on handling criticism is excellent material for church leaders!"

Joseph Castleberry, president, Northwest University
and author of The Kingdom Net

"From the pen of a talented and respected pastor and state and national church official comes a definitive work on how to respond to and personally handle criticism. *When Words Hurt* draws from many biblical characters, present day circumstances, and the author's vast personal experiences to illustrate how to respond to criticism with nobility, diplomacy, and discretion. Any person leading a church organization, governmental or private concern, or even their own family will find godly wisdom from Dr. Warren Bullock on this timeless but relevant subject."

Drexel T. Brunson, president, Empower Resources International, Inc. and
author of The Servant Organization for Jesus

"We all face criticism at one time or another and many of us are criticized often. In fact, the more high profile your position of leadership is, the more often you will be criticized. Dr. Warren Bullock has modeled well for us how to deal with criticism over the course of his life and shares his wonderful insight with us in *When Words Hurt*. I have greatly benefitted personally from Warren's leadership and consider him a true friend and partner in ministry. I highly recommend this book to everyone who has ever been criticized, which according to my research, is everyone!"

Rick Ross, lead pastor, First Assembly of God, Concord, North Carolina

"Warren Bullock is so well qualified to write this book, not because he is critical but because he is eminently blessed to help those who are. He is my friend, a friend of my family, and a friend of God. Nothing is better said than that! I bought the first 150 copies to give to my friends: I just wish I had more friends so that I could buy more books."

Sam Johnson, executive director, Priority One

"You will either respond to your critics by design or default. *When Words Hurt* will engage, inspire, and motivate you to find the best and highest design for handling the harsh and hurtful words that come your way. This book is a superb extension of Warren Bullock's wisdom and substance. Get your hands on this important book and start being a relational change agent in your family, your community, or your organization. Trust me—you'll never look at the critic and their criticism in the same way again."

Kent Ingle, President of Southeastern University and author of *9 Disciplines of Enduring Leadership*

"How should a pastor or leader respond to unkind criticism and mean-spirited remarks? Drawn from decades serving as successful pastor, denominational executive, and leader, Dr. Warren Bullock has written a practical, Bible anchored guide. He shares excellent concepts and procedures drawn from real church experiences that will help pastors/leaders calm troubled emotional waters. In my judgment, every leader should have this book as a ready reference and resource."

Don Argue, former president, National Association of Evangelicals and Ambassador at Large for Convoy of Hope

"Having had the pleasure to work closely with Dr. Warren Bullock over the years and examine his leadership up close and personal, I can assure you that he speaks from personal experience. During seasons of prosperity and adversity I've observed Warren exemplify the themes of this book: grace, character, competency, chemistry, and calling. In these pages you will read an honest man's journey and life lessons for *When Words Hurt*. With compelling stories, practical instruction, and biblical integrity, Warren provides insight to increase our own self-awareness and understand our reactions. At the same time, he offers discerning counsel about if, when, and how to respond to the critic's words. I discovered much to glean and use, and so will you."

Don Detrick, associate leader, Northwest Ministry Network,
Assemblies of God and author of *Growing Disciples Organically.*

When Words ~~Hurt~~

Helping Godly Leaders Respond Wisely to Criticism

Warren D. Bullock

SALUBRIS
RESOURCES

When Words Hurt

Copyright © 2015 by Warren D. Bullock

ALL RIGHTS RESERVED

Published by Salubris Resources
1445 N. Boonville Ave.
Springfield, Missouri 65802
www.salubrisresources.com

Cover design by Sheepish Design (www.sheepishdesign.org)
Interior design by Tom Shumaker

Produced with the assistance of Livingstone, the Publishing Services Division of Barton-Veerman Company (www.livingstonecorp.com). Project staff includes: Bruce Barton, Ashley Taylor, and Tom Shumaker.

NOTE: Some of the names in this book, as well as some identifying details, have been changed to protect the anonymity of the people involved.

ISBN: 978-1-68067-042-4

Printed in the United States of America

18 17 16 15 • 1 2 3 4 5

Dedicated to my son,
Jeffrey D. Bullock,
and my daughter,
Natasha L. Martinez,
who are my pride and joy.

Contents

Foreword

If you are an educator, spouse, parent, pastor, or leader in the market place, you will find *When Words Hurt* extremely practical and thought provoking. Recently, I received a scathing email from someone close to me. It hurt! There is nothing enjoyable about opening your inbox and reading harsh criticisms. How does one respond? How does one answer a critic, particularly if there might be a kernel of truth in the criticism? Should you listen to criticism, or disregard it all together? How does one live with the reality of receiving criticism . . . without developing a calloused heart?

When Words Hurt answers these questions and offers strong insights for dealing with both the criticism—and the critic! Dr. Bullock's insights are invaluable for dealing with the negative feedback. This book is an indispensable read for leaders of all fields.

Aristotle said that the only way to avoid criticism is to "say nothing, do nothing, be nothing." The issue isn't will you receive criticism, but how will you react to it when you do? The natural response is to get defensive, dismiss the feedback, or internalize the words of the critic, causing hurt, discouragement, and a heart filled with pain. Eventually, criticism may even paralyze, preventing leaders from effectively accomplishing their mission. Unfounded or even founded criticism has caused the miscarriage of many great dreams. By providing principles and down-to-earth skills for coping with critics and criticism, Dr. Bullock equips us with the tools necessary to "stay focused" on our tasks, not our detractors.

Dr. Bullock skillfully grounds his thoughts with a biblical foundation. His insights are not born from a "self-help" perspective but substantiated with well thought out scriptural examples and personal insights. He draws illustrations and insights from biblical characters who had to deal with criticism . . . including Jesus.

Dr. Bullock also writes from life experiences, sharing personal stories that exemplify the humility and strength vital for leaders to cope with criticism. His authentic and honest approach to criticism is truly refreshing. Just reading his mishaps when dealing with criticism is worth your time! Responding with a gentle answer is more than a philosophical reflex for Dr. Bullock. For him, it is a practical step of obedience, and a tangible undertaking of love.

Warren Bullock exemplifies a life of grace. His unique definition of grace, "God's goodness to people who don't deserve it," is reflected in every story and on every page of this book. Grace enables leaders to overlook people's careless words and show mercy, even as God shows us mercy. As you read this book, allow the Spirit of God to bring healing to past wounds and insights in dealing with future criticism. Spend some time reflecting on the Points to Ponder at the end of each chapter, allowing God to infuse grace into your life.

Dr. Troy Jones, lead pastor, New Life Church, Renton, Washington

Introduction

Social media has transformed relational communications. In the past if my children weren't home and I needed to talk with them, I would call them. Now, if I want or need a quick response from them, I text them. For the younger generation(s), even email has become out of fashion.

Unfortunately, I can't keep up with the breaking trends in electronic communication. Change happens so quickly that I'm always behind. Just yesterday I heard on the news that the number of users of Instagram has now passed Twitter. I have no idea what that means! Some apps now allow anonymous comments, good or bad, about targeted individuals. What's next?

Nonstop cable news provides up-to-date news coverage but also offers instant analysis of events and people. For instance, every decision made by the President of the United States is immediately examined from every possible angle. Those who agree with presidential decisions today may well find themselves in disagreement with tomorrow's decisions. But we can count on this: Whatever the President does will be criticized. (Wouldn't you just love to be the President?)

When I watch my favorite football team, the Seattle Seahawks, the "color man" will examine every play in detail. A re-run and/or slo-mo of the play will be discussed with both positive and negative comments. In the course of the game, key players, coaches, owners, and game plans will be thoroughly scrutinized. What we hear is only an opinion by one person, and it may be wrong, but he's paid to provide his perspective, insights, and criticism.

Good people are hired to criticize. So we have movie critics, restaurant critics, book critics, etc. In fact, on social media I can be a critic in all of those areas. I just don't get paid for it.

Recently the multi-media company, Sony, was hacked and embarrassing emails from top executives were revealed. Some of their comments about so-called stars were less than complimentary, and the executives were criticized for their unkind barbs. Old emails never die!

It isn't uncommon for Christians to read articles, blogs, and books, or to hear messages and exhortations about the good and evil use of the tongue. James 3 is often cited because of its warnings about the devastation the tongue can cause. "The tongue also is a fire, a world of evil. . . . It corrupts the whole person . . . and is itself set on fire by hell. . . . It is a restless evil, full of deadly poison" (3:6, 8). Despite the conveniences of social media, the tongue is our first and foremost means of communication—and criticism.

Proverbs also reminds us that "the tongue has the power of life and death" (18:21). Good speech produces positive benefits, but hurtful, negative words create relational distance and hard-to-heal wounds. Words have power, causing either unbelievable pain or helpful encouragement. We understand this, not only because it's what the Word teaches, but because of our own personal experience.

But such life experience rarely prepares us for those occasions when harsh words are aimed at us. When sharply critical words have hurt us, we flounder for remedies that will ease the pain. What antidotes are there when our hearts ache? How should we respond when verbal barbs find their mark? Do we respond the same way to every criticism? Do we respond at all? What *is* a Christian response to criticism?

That's what *When Words Hurt* is about. Its purpose is to provide Christian leaders with biblically sound responses that limit the damage criticism creates, reduce the hurt it causes, and help to restore relationships it has broken.

I've learned some of these responses by being the target of criticism. I confess that at times I have reacted inappropriately, but the Lord has used even my failures to continue my schooling in the Spirit. Other times the Lord has helped me to respond in a way that honored Him. I'm still a stumbling pilgrim when it comes to dealing with critical remarks aimed at me.

Observing how others have responded to criticism also provides us with learning lessons. The Scripture is filled with such examples.

Outside the biblical text other great leaders have modeled grace under fire, and we can learn from them as well.

Biblical principles guide us unerringly in our quest for good responses to our critics. They are universally applicable to all and are deeply rooted in grace. Grace is commonly defined as *unmerited favor*. My definition of grace is *God's goodness to people who don't deserve it.*

When we are criticized, the person who least deserves grace is the critic. And that is exactly the point. We offer what they don't deserve in the same way God offers it to us. As grace has liberated us, so responses filled with grace will bring freedom and release to both the criticized and the criticizer.

o   o   o   o

CHAPTER

1

. . . .

Every Leader's Challenge

*"A great door for effective work has opened to me,
and there are many who oppose me."*
1 Corinthians 16:9

The choice to lead something . . . opens you up to a world of pain.
—Ruth Haley Barton

When I was just a little guy, probably six or seven years of age, I
loved to "play" church. The congregation consisted of my older sister,
two cousins who lived down the street, and me. We actually played
dual roles; we were the congregation and the leaders/pastors. So we
would take turns at the various aspects of a church service. One would
lead the songs that we all knew by heart. Then someone would lead in
prayer. If the prayer was particularly inspiring, we would also pray for
the sick—each other—even though we were all healthy. Finally one of
us would preach. We never preached very long because our audience
had a very short attention span. After the message we would give the
altar call, and someone in the audience of three would raise their hand
for prayer and come to the altar to accept Jesus as their Savior. Over
time each of us was saved several times.

My oldest cousin was the best preacher. He had a way with words,
"the gift of gab," as we used to say. He could string out a Bible story
with inventive and imaginative embellishments. Even though I was
very young, once in a while they let me preach. I don't remember now

what I said; it was probably a mishmash of everything I had heard my pastor-father say in the pulpit.

After our little church service was over, we would critique one another on how we could have done better, especially the preaching. Once after I had been the preacher, my sister and older cousin were quite direct in their criticism and it hurt my feelings. I had done my best, and it seemed like they didn't appreciate it very much. I struggled to stifle the tears that threatened to slide down my cheeks. So they tried to soften their not-too-subtle barbs by attributing my inadequacies to my young age. After all, they were two whole years older than I, and thus so much more experienced.

Isn't it interesting that when I page through my photo album of memories, the pictures about our playtime are fuzzy and distant, but the snapshot of peer criticism is as sharp and clear as if I had just taken it on my iPhone? I could have received ten compliments, but what clings to my memory are words that were less than complimentary.

When you're on the front lines of battle, you're going to get shot at. No leader is exempt.

What makes criticism stick in our minds like verbal velcro? It reminds me of the burrs that used to stick to my pants when I played in a weed patch. Criticism is like that.

This childhood experience with my sister and cousins was perhaps my first lesson in leadership: *Leaders get criticized*. And guess what? Nothing has changed. Leaders still get criticized. It goes with the territory. When you're on the front lines of battle, you're going to get shot at. No leader is exempt. Some verbal arrows will find their mark. We will be wounded; it's inevitable. So we shouldn't be shocked when it happens.

You Are a Leader

If you're thinking, "That may be true, but it doesn't apply to me because I'm not a leader," think again. You're a leader if anyone is following you. Do you have children, grandchildren, students, co-workers, friends, or associates? If so, someone is following you. You *are* a leader. Unfortunately that means you'll be criticized.

A classic definition of leadership states that leadership is influence. Each of us has some degree of influence. The apostle Paul reminds us that "none of us lives to himself alone and none of us dies to himself alone" (Rom. 14:7). Our sphere of influence is probably greater than we understand, which means we are leading those we influence. Consequently criticism is going to come our way. The question is, "How are we going to handle it?"

We don't all travel the same paths to places of leadership. Some paths are more like trails with twist and turns, underbrush and obstacles. They are arduous, challenging, and often undefined. Other paths seem more like freeways clogged with traffic; it takes a long time to get to our destination. Some paths to leadership may be slowed by traffic lights. They require stopping and starting, and take lots of energy. We may face detours along the way. Occasionally, we hit a dead end and have to turn around and find the path again. But, eventually, our place of leadership will come into view.

Here are some, but certainly not all, of the paths to leadership. By the time we finish reviewing them, I hope you are convinced that you are a leader.

Marriage

When a couple is happily united in marriage, they both instantly become leaders. The husband leads some aspects of the home, and the wife leads others. Consequently, when one leads, whether husband or wife, the other follows. Hence the Bible encourages married couples to "submit to one another out of reverence for Christ" (Eph. 5:21).

Parenthood

Is there any more important leadership role than parenting? Dad and Mom are a child's greatest influencers. Parents give a child direction through systematic, intentional instruction and discipline. But parents are also models for handling life with all its hairpin turns and ups and downs.

Have you ever seen a toddler trying to walk with his little feet in Daddy's big shoes? How about little girls dressing up in Mommy's clothes and high heels? We laugh at their playful efforts to be grown up, but something deeper is going on. Could these little ones be saying, "I want to be just like my Daddy or my Mommy"? Probably so. And most parents have realized that their influence is still required even after the kids leave home.

Position

When a postman is promoted to postmaster, that person assumes a leadership role with greater responsibilities because of the new position. The manager of a hardware store has more responsibility by virtue of his position than the stock boy does. A teacher is positioned for broad and lasting influence, both by what is taught and through the multiplication process inherent in teaching many different students.

Position doesn't make anyone a leader, but position is the recognition and affirmation of leadership. Some positions have more influence and power than others. The office of president of the United States is certainly far more influential than almost any other position in our country. Yet in the position *you* hold, there is leadership influence.

Education

One doesn't need an education to be a leader, but it helps. My father insisted, even demanded, that I attend Bible college before entering his profession—vocational ministry. So I was the first in our immediate family to earn a bachelor's degree. That didn't mean I was smarter than my Dad, but it did mean I was better prepared to be a minister than he had been at my age, a fact that delighted him.

Education compresses knowledge into a tighter learning timeframe than life experience. When knowledge is gained only through life-lessons and self-instruction, it takes much longer. Also, when others know your educational background, this enhances your credibility and expands your potential for effective leadership.

Credentials

Getting professional credentials often follows education. When I go to the doctor's office, I want to see certificates and diplomas on the wall that validate my physician's education, areas of specialization, and expertise. When I'm under a doctor's care, he's the leader. He tells me what I need to do to achieve and maintain good health. His credentials remind me that he's the medical authority, not me.

The Gift of Leadership

Some people are natural leaders. When our son Jeff was eleven or twelve years old, I asked him to mow the lawn in the backyard. That was not a task he particularly enjoyed. In that he was much like his Dad! A few minutes later I looked out our patio window and was dismayed to see him sitting on the picnic table. Then I saw three or four of his neighborhood friends, and to my amazement they were taking turns doing the mowing. He had rounded them up and challenged them to see how fast they could make a circuit of the lawn with the mower. To increase the incentive he sat on the picnic table timing them. I don't know who won the mowing contest, but Jeff exhibited leadership even at that young age, though not in a way I would have anticipated. He was, and still is, a leader. By the way, I wouldn't recommend him or his crew to be your landscapers.

It would be fun at this point to debate whether leaders are born or developed. Good arguments can be marshaled on both sides of the issue. However the Bible makes it clear that the Holy Spirit endows some believers with the gift of leadership. "We have different gifts, according to the grace given us. . . . If it is leadership, let him govern diligently" (Rom.12:6–8). The Greek word for *leadership* means to guide with care.[1] There's little question that this is an active gift in the lives of many Christ-followers. The gift may find expression through position, may be enhanced through education, and validated by credentials, but the source of the gift is the Holy Spirit who gives the gifts "just as he determines" (1 Cor. 12:11).

Pastors

The word *pastor* is not mentioned frequently in Scripture, but *shepherd* is often used. They are one and the same; the word for shepherd is also the word for pastor. So the apostle Paul told the Ephesian elders, "Be shepherds of the church of God" (Acts 20:28). Of course one of the primary tasks of the shepherd is to lead the flock, just as our Good Shepherd leads us beside quiet waters. Sheep without a shepherd will be scattered and set upon by wolves. They will get hungry from lack of food without a shepherd to lead them to green pastures. Of all that a pastor is to be and do, he must be a leader of God's flock.

Calling

Among the highest aspirations of the believer is the desire to live life completely in the will of God, fulfilling His holy purposes daily. We know that beyond the call to salvation, God has called each of us to a unique destiny that provides personal fulfillment, fosters kingdom extension, and brings glory to God. Whatever our calling in God's will may be, we live with a sense that divine providence is guiding us.

We aren't too shocked when those outside the circle of faith find fault and gossip, but when supposedly good Christians aim their verbal weapons at us, we may be caught off guard.

When we follow the leadership of our great Shepherd, we experience the realization of our destiny.

So are you convinced now that you are a leader? I hope so, because that's the good news. Now get ready for some bad news.

Leaders Get Criticized

Yes, as a leader you are going to get your share of criticism. We aren't too shocked when those outside the circle of faith find fault and gossip, but when supposedly good Christians aim their verbal weapons at us, we may be caught off guard. We assume that since all of us are on the same team, every team member will support the others. Unfortunately, we learn that our assumption is not true, and we can feel betrayed, sabotaged, and angry. "What is one to *do* with the people pains involved in leadership?"[2]

Having worked with hundreds of Christian leaders, I've discovered that many seem dismayed to learn that serving Jesus and fulfilling their calling is extremely hard, painful, and demanding. Yet we follow the One who said, "If anyone would come after me, he must deny himself and take up his cross daily and follow me" (Luke 9:23). The way of the cross requires us to affirm, "I have been crucified with Christ and I no longer live, but Christ lives in me" (Gal. 2:20). We are challenged to "endure hardship . . . like a good soldier of Christ Jesus" (2 Tim. 2:3).

So why do we seem so surprised when leadership is tough? Why does criticism throw us off our game? Why do we keep expecting bouquets instead of brickbats? We must accept what the late Edwin Friedman said: "Criticism of the leader (which is a form of sabotage) is so predictable that it should be viewed as part and parcel of the leadership process itself."[3]

Confirmation of this principle can be readily observed in the lives of biblical leaders.

Joseph

His brothers didn't just criticize him, "they hated him and could not speak a kind word to him" (Gen. 37:4). You can almost hear the contempt in their voices, "Here comes the dreamer. . . . Let's kill him" (Gen. 37:19–20). So much for family love and loyalty!

Moses

Leading the children of Israel was like the proverbial "herding of cats." They rarely were happy with Moses' leadership and were not shy about letting him know it. They grumbled, complained, griped, and moaned about their imagined misery, most of which they blamed on their leader.

Samuel

After a long and fruitful ministry, Samuel was rejected by Israel, who demanded a king instead. He was not criticized for what he had done, but for what he was never going to be—a king.

David

Despite his amazing victory over Goliath, David was pursued by King Saul who wanted to kill him. His own "band of brothers" wanted to stone him at Ziklag. Even his son Absalom undermined him, chased him from the city of David, slept with his concubines, and fought him for the kingship.

Elijah

King Ahab called Elijah names: "You troubler of Israel" (1 Kings 18:17). Queen Jezebel assassinated many of the prophets of God, and threatened to do the same to Elijah. He was so intimidated he had suicidal thoughts, except he didn't want to do the deed himself—he wanted God to do it for him!

Paul

Criticism seems to have been the least of Paul's concerns. Listen to some of the mental, emotional, and spiritual challenges he noted in 2 Corinthians 1 and 4:

- Suffered hardships
- Hard-pressed
- Perplexed
- Persecuted
- Struck down
- Under great pressure
- Despaired even of life
- Felt the sentence of death

This litany of pain and adversity doesn't include the physical wounds he received. It's certain that in addition to all of these trials, he confronted criticism of his life and ministry.

So if people criticized these spiritual giants, if these whom we mark as great leaders had their detractors, why would we expect to be any different? Accept it. Leaders get criticized.

We should be encouraged by Paul's perception of ministry. "Since through God's mercy we have this ministry, we do not lose heart" (2 Cor. 4:1). He wasn't just talking about vocational ministry but about ministry that every Christian has. Such ministries are given to us as an act of God's mercy. That's good to remember when we are assailed by unkind and untrue words. God doesn't grant us these ministries because He is mad at us and wants to see us suffer. He is merciful to us.

Paul seems to be saying, among other things, that inherent in ministry is the mercy necessary to deal with the barrage of criticism that is bound to come. So we don't lose heart. Mercy that brought us into our ministry is mercy enough to help us endure the verbal buffeting we will experience. The bad news that leaders get criticized becomes the good news that God's mercy is more than adequate to help us get through it.

Points to Ponder

1. Think for a few moments about who you lead. Perhaps list the names of those who see you as a leader and thus follow your leadership, example, and direction. Call each of their names in prayer, or if it is a large following, say prayers for the whole group.

2. Is your ministry calling clear? Do the roles you now play fulfill or contradict that call? Could you be receiving criticism because your labors are not in keeping with your calling? Through the Word, the guidance of the Spirit, the counsel and confirmation of godly people you respect, seek to clarify what your calling and kingdom-destiny are.

3. If you are presently under attack by critics, in prayer ask God—

   - To give you deep inner peace despite the turmoil;
   - To help you maintain a Christ-like attitude toward your critics;
   - To guard your heart against resentment and anger;
   - To provide spiritual protection for family members who may be feeling the ripple effect of the criticism.

4. Memorize Psalm 19:14: "May the words of my mouth and the meditation of my heart be pleasing in your sight, O LORD, my Rock and my Redeemer."

5. In what ways has your ministry provided mercy in your life?

o o o o

CHAPTER

2

. . . .
Analysis of a Critic

"For out of the overflow of the heart the mouth speaks."
Matthew 12:34

There are many people who will try to stand in your way, even cut you off at the knees, but it is often more about them than about you.—Katie Couric

My annual physical exam is *not* the highlight of my year! I've been through it often enough to know I will be poked, prodded, weighed, tested, and examined.

I especially don't like getting weighed. After checking in, my first stop is always at the scales. I feel like a boxer weighing in before a fight. To be fair, someone else should have to weigh-in too. Maybe the doctor. Or what if the nurse also had to step on the scales after I did? It wouldn't be long before the weigh-in would be a practice of the past. I've noticed, too, that the doctor's scales always weigh heavier than my scales at home. I suspect it's a medical conspiracy to get me to diet!

When I finally get to a private room to wait for the doctor, I just start to relax when the nurse purposefully approaches with a long needle. My relaxation is over. Needles and blood-draws make me cringe. Sucking out a person's life-blood may be popular in vampire movies, but I don't have to like it when it's happening in real time. Occasionally, it takes the nurse several "pokes" in my arm before the needle finds a good vein. I hate when that happens.

In spite of my misgivings about the whole process, I still faithfully schedule my physical each year. I have an excellent doctor, and certainly my exam is necessary, even though I approach it with a certain amount of dread.

Since I've had occasional heart problems, the exam nearly always includes an electrocardiogram (EKG). If you've had such a test, you know it doesn't take long and, thank goodness, it doesn't involve needles. Ten small electrode patches are attached to the skin of your chest, arms, and legs. The computer then creates a picture on graph paper of the electrical impulses traveling through your heart. A similar test can be done while you walk on the treadmill. It's aptly called a stress test. A physician, especially a cardiologist, is skilled in interpreting your readout to determine if there are any problematic issues.

But heart problems aren't all physical. Some are spiritual. When a verbal volcano erupts, pouring out hot words that inflict pain on others, it reveals a heart problem. A spiritual EKG is needed. We believe the truth of Jesus' words that "out of the overflow of the heart the mouth speaks" (Matt. 12:34). So when someone unleashes a barrage of criticism, we know they have a heart condition that needs addressing. Yet they may not see the connection between their words and their heart.

So what is the heart diagnosis? What abnormality of the heart causes such attacks? What do the negative symptoms reveal about root causes?

Let's be honest. If left to ourselves without the help of the Holy Spirit, we really can't answer those questions because we don't know our own hearts. "The heart is deceitful above all things and beyond cure. Who can understand it?" (Jer. 17:9).

I got a call one day from a man who was having a marital crisis. He wanted to meet with me as soon as possible. I knew him quite well and had observed that as a professed Christian he was seemingly circumspect in his behavior. But now he confessed that for several months he had been having an ongoing affair; he had been unfaithful to his wife. His conclusion about his conduct was revealing: "I don't understand it. I am not that kind of person." He didn't know his own heart. He was deceived into thinking his heart was purer than it actually was. I reminded him that all of us are capable of sinful behavior when we don't allow God to keep our hearts clean.

An obscure Old Testament character named Hazael illustrates our failure to truly know our own hearts. In Hazael's case, a prophet perceived the heart issues that he was blind to.

Hazael had been sent by Ben-Hadad, king of Aram, to the prophet Elijah. The king was sick and wanted Hazael to inquire on his behalf whether he would recover. The prophet responded by affirming that indeed the king would recover from his affliction. "Elisha then stared hard at Hazael, *reading his heart.* . . . Then the Holy Man wept" (2 Kings 8:10, *The Message*, emphasis mine). When Hazael questioned him about his tears, Elisha began to prophetically outline the terrible atrocities Hazael would commit against Israel.

- -

Sometimes, criticism isn't about a lack of intellectual brilliance but a lack of information.

- -

Hazael seemed offended by this prediction and responded, "Am I a mongrel dog that I'd do such a horrible thing" (2 Kings 8:13, *The Message*)? In other words, "Who? Me?" He was clueless as to the true condition of his heart, but the prophet saw what Hazael couldn't see: In the depths of his heart he was evil. When Hazael went home, he assassinated the king, and ascended to the throne. Later in his reign he initiated the horrific outbreaks of violence and cruelty that more than fulfilled Elisha's prophecy.

Have words popped out of your mouth that have caused you to think, "Where did that come from?" Or maybe you've said, "I didn't really mean to say that!" Actually, you did. It was in your heart all the time. You just didn't know it. If criticism consistently pours unhindered from your mouth, you need a spiritual EKG to help you know the condition of your heart.

So if criticism comes from the heart, what conditions of the heart create it? I'm not a psychologist or psychiatrist. Probing into someone's psyche is not my expertise. However, I am a student of human behavior, and have been the recipient of my share of criticism. So these observations come from my own experience.

Ignorance

By citing ignorance as a prompter of criticism, my intention is not to demean anyone's intelligence. But sometimes, criticism isn't about a lack of intellectual brilliance but a lack of information. Critics have not always heard "the rest of the story." Their supposed omniscience has information gaps. Their snide or unkind comments may be the product of a lack of information or misinformation. They are not privy to the big picture. Consequently their criticism is founded in ignorance. The leader will do well to ignore them and their negative comments.

Some aspects of leadership and decision-making may require a limited dissemination of information. For instance, when I decided to release a pastoral staff member from their responsibilities, I couldn't usually give the congregation all the causes of dismissal. To do so would have impugned the staff member's character or competence. I refused to criticize that person as a means of justifying my decision. That refusal meant that I would become the target of criticism for my actions because I was unable and unwilling to provide the church with all the evidence. Sometimes those members loyal to the staff pastor left the church. Sometimes the dismissed pastor spread disinformation about his release from employment. These things only confirmed that my decision to dismiss that person was correct. But if the faults and foibles of the staff pastor are not fully exposed, then criticism from others will be based on their inability to see the whole picture, to be privy to all the information.

When information is withheld out of self-interest, a leader may deserve the criticism he gets. The big picture isn't always something to be held back. Full disclosure, even when it makes the leader look less than stellar, can defuse a lot of verbal potshots. The leader's transparency will score points in the minds of many, despite failures he may need to admit. However those points depend on the nature of the failures.

Recognize that when others don't know what you know, you may be the target for criticism. However such criticism can be blunted if you are able to provide clear explanations.

Superiority

Even when all the facts are laid out, leaders still get criticized. Lack of information isn't the cause, but a sense of superiority may be. Some people are convinced that they know better than the leader—any leader—what ought to happen, how it should happen, and who should make it happen. This rises from an attitude of, "If I were the leader . . . If it were my decision . . . If I were in charge."

- -

We still have among us those who purport to have ascended spiritual escalators that exalt them to lofty heights above the rank and file.

- -

Their imagined superiority makes them champion second-guessers. They excel at undercutting the leader. They foment dissension. They do the leader "a great deal of harm" (2 Tim. 4:14), just as Alexander the metalworker did to Paul. Alexander also strongly opposed Paul's message, which was even more serious. It's one thing to oppose the leader, and quite another thing to oppose a word God has sent. Paul's urgent challenge to Timothy still makes a lot of sense: "Be on your guard" (2 Tim. 4:15).

Those Paul called "super-apostles" were a constant menace to him and the church (2 Cor. 11:6; 12:11). We still have among us those who purport to have ascended spiritual escalators that exalt them to lofty heights above the rank and file. Therefore, they assume that the most notable positions should be theirs. From that elevated platform they assume that their critical pronouncements transcend all others and are worthy to be heard.

These critics often sink under the weight of their own press releases.

The Lord has a way of clearly revealing the cracks in their character. Their impact can be hurtful, but their influence will be temporary.

Insecurity

Isn't it sometimes true that a person who projects a superior attitude is trying to cover up or compensate for personal insecurities? If we're honest, all of us must admit to being insecure in some way. Finding fault is one coping mechanism for insecurity. We attempt to make others look bad, so we'll look better. E. Stanley Jones reminds us, "Religious people are in the business of endeavoring to be good. They are therefore tempted to point out the faults of others, so that by implication they themselves may appear better. It is a miserable business."[4] Indeed it is.

Jesus pointedly asked, "Why do you look at the speck of sawdust in your brother's eye and pay no attention to the plank in your own eye?" (Matt. 7:3). This hyperbole is absurd enough to make us chuckle, but while we're smiling about our critics dealing with a big piece of lumber in their eyes, Jesus' question pierces our own insecure hearts.

. . . .

We can't meet everyone's expectations. People's expectations are often greater than God's expectations!

. . . .

All of us, whatever our insecurities, do well to heed our Lord's advice, "First take the plank out of your own eye, and then you will see clearly to remove the speck from your brother's eye." (Matt. 7:5).

Expectations

Every job description outlines what is expected of an employee. But the worker soon learns that there are unwritten expectations beyond what has been clearly prescribed. The norms of corporate culture dictate behavior beyond the job description. The "direct report" may expect job outcomes that were not even mentioned at hiring time. Job evaluations may overflow with criticism for failure to meet nebulous standards that were never enunciated.

In nearly every new leadership position I've held, there was someone who wanted and expected to be my buddy. They had the expectation that they would immediately become part of my inner circle and be privy to my inmost thoughts and private issues. These so-called buddies were nearly always disappointed. My inner circle of very close friends is small, and I want to choose who they are, without being pressured to include someone I don't trust. So I didn't meet their expectations, and sometimes they later criticized and undercut me.

Face it! We can't meet everyone's expectations. People's expectations are often greater than God's expectations! When we fail to meet their expectations, criticism can result. However, we're only obligated to fulfill God's expectations. And thankfully, His yoke is easy and His burden is light (Matt. 11:30).

Control

As a denominational leader, I've been called upon to serve as a church trouble-shooter. In my own mind and heart I've recast this role from trouble-shooter to peacemaker. In seeking to mediate church disputes I believe that most often the core issue is control. Most internal control squabbles could be distilled to two questions. First, what kind of church are we going to become? Second, who makes that decision?

The conflict usually begins with an important decision. For example the pastor decides to stop having a traditional service that appeals to seniors. Disagreement with and criticism of the decision is immediate and vehement. The pastor's rationale is that the church needs to appeal to a younger generation. The seniors protest that they not only disagree with the decision, but they are dismayed that they had no say in the decision.

The central issue is, what kind of church are we going to become? A church that makes an attempt to accommodate seniors or appeals to a new generation? Then the decision-making process comes into question. Who makes the decision that maintains the same course or charts a new direction? Behind all of it is the issue of control.

If you dig deeper, control issues are closely linked to change.

• Where there is change, there is resistance.
• Where there is resistance, there is criticism.
• Habitual critics resists change, because they're losing control.

But it is also true that—

• There is no growth without change. Our growing children and grandchildren prove that.
• There is no change without pain. That's why we resist it so fiercely.
• There is no maturity without growth. And our destiny is to grow into Jesus' likeness.

This chapter is not focused on explaining the relationship between resistance, criticism, growth, change, and maturity. However, on these issues critics speak out of both sides of their mouths. They quickly affirm their desire to be like Jesus and see the kingdom advance, but they actively resist and criticize the changes that make spiritual progress possible. It's all about control.

Rebellion

This criticism-prompter isn't always immediately evident. Rebellion can hide behind the facade of religious respectability. It wears the mask of seeming spirituality, but it can't be kept hidden forever.

A pastor friend, whom I'll call Bob, kept his mask in place for years until the Holy Spirit pulled it off. He has given me permission to share his story.

Bob arrived late to a district-wide ministers' meeting moderated by one of the denominational leaders. As Bob and a friend found their seats, he whispered a comment about the leader that was so snide and cutting he could hardly believe it came out of his mouth. It was the direct fulfillment of Psalm 64:3–4: "They sharpen their tongues like swords and aim their words like deadly arrows. They shoot from ambush at the innocent man; they shoot at him suddenly, without fear."

His sharp, cutting words evoked immediate and deep conviction. He told me, "It was like the Holy Spirit drove a spear into my heart." It was indeed a spiritual EKG that revealed his true self. His words and the Spirit helped him recognize an inner rebellion against authority. He began to weep and repent as he saw himself through the eyes of the Spirit.

Bob was the lead pastor of a growing turnaround church. The church had been at low ebb when he took over, but it had undergone remarkable change and the growth seemed positive and encouraging.

One of John Maxwell's *21 Irrefutable Laws of Leadership* is: Who you are is whom you attract. This rebellious pastor was attracting people

. . . .

It isn't uncommon for people who wound with words to have been wounded themselves.

. . . .

to his church who also had rebellious hearts. He was a magnet for unrepentant Christians like himself who refused to submit to authority. The church was growing, but the church was not healthy.

After the pastor repented, he invited the denomination leader to preach at his church. He not only stopped criticizing those in authority over him, but began working cooperatively with them. Can you guess what many of the newcomers to his church did? Yes, they rebelled against him. They tried to evict him from his position, and when that didn't succeed, scores of the rebellious people began to leave the church. It caused him unbelievable pain, but he would not, and did not, revert to his old rebellious and critical ways.

Not every critic is convicted by what they say like Bob was. But their words reveal a heart condition that is personally destructive, that "slices and dices" other people, and blocks positive advances.

Woundedness

It isn't uncommon for people who wound with words to have been wounded themselves. Perhaps they've been verbally or physically abused. Perhaps the wounds of a nasty divorce have not healed. Betrayal by a friend may have left painful scars. Out of their pain-filled souls they lash out at others, slashing with hurtful words. They may not always understand what triggers their outburst, but woundedness lies behind it. The abused often becomes the abuser.

Esau's wound was self-inflicted. He willingly sold his birthright to his brother, Jacob. When Jacob deceived his father into giving him Esau's blessing as well, this multiplied the wounds. Esau's grudge morphed into revenge, and he intended to kill Jacob after his father's death. But his anger was also directed at his mother and father, Rebekah and Isaac. She had been a co-conspirator with Jacob in the deceit, and he had fallen for their charade.

When Esau learned that Jacob had been sent away in part so he wouldn't marry a Canaanite woman, what did he do? He did what would hurt his parents the most. He married a Canaanite, the daughter of Ishmael. Why? He was deeply wounded.

Being wounded doesn't excuse Esau or anyone else for hurtful words, but it may help us better understand why they say the things they do.

The Wrong Target

Psalm 69, which has Messianic undertones, is a cry to God from David's heart. His enemies were assailing him, and he longed for deliverance. David lamented, "The insults of those who insult you fall on me" (Ps. 69:9). This very personal exclamation enunciates a leadership principle common among Christians: When people don't know how to target God with their insults, grievances, and anger, they target His followers instead.

I've been amazed over the years at the number of people who are mad at God. He gets blamed for a multitude of offenses.

- He didn't keep my mother from dying.
- He could have prevented that head-on collision.
- Where was He when the cupboards were bare, and I had nothing to feed my kids?

• He's supposed to answer prayer, but when I pray, He's silent.
• What about all the starving children? Why doesn't He do something for them?

Angry at God. But since they can't see Him, touch Him, or force Him to answer them, they aim their arrows at His representatives.

The nation of Israel wasn't dissatisfied or critical of Samuel's leadership, but at the end of his life they clamored for a king. They didn't want a judge, a prophet, or one of Samuel's sons. A king was all that would satisfy them. Samuel was disheartened and displeased. But the Lord assured him, "It is not you they have rejected, but they have rejected me as their king" (1 Sam. 8:7). In other words, "Samuel, it's not about you and your leadership. It's about Me, and their attitude toward My kingship over them."

Criticism can be like that. It seems aimed at us, but the real target is our Lord. This shouldn't take us by surprise. Since we're one with Him, united with Him through the cross, we share the pain of unkind words no matter whom they are aimed at. Perhaps this is a small part of what the apostle Paul calls "the fellowship of sharing in his sufferings" (Phil. 3:10). What hurts Him, hurts us, and the pain we feel causes Him pain as well.

Even when we think we understand why people criticize, the barbs still smart. Could it be that God allows these wounds, large and small, to be one of His tools in refining our characters?

During my high school years I worked at a print shop that also published a weekly newspaper. This was long before the development of desktop publishing or publishing software. So my primary task was to run the linotype, which produced copy for the newspaper on lead "slugs." Pictures were transformed into lead as well. Headlines were handset using movable type. We put it all together in forms that were then installed on the press, and we hand-fed the paper into the press. Presto, an eight-page newspaper.

Once the newspaper was printed and delivered, we had to gather all the used lead for melting. That was my least favorite job. Lead is very heavy, and I had to lug it to a big container (think witch's caldron), dump it in, and light the gas burner under it. After about four hours, the lead would be melted. But that wasn't good enough because it had ink, dirt, paper, and other debris mixed in with the lead. So I would squirt oil into the lead, throw a match on top, and it would burn the accumulated dross. Then I would scrape the dross off for disposal.

After all of that you would think the lead would be clean. Not so. If I stirred it up again, more dross would come to the top. No matter how many times I removed the dross, if I stirred it again, I would get more dross. Finally when I felt like it was reasonably clean, I would dip it out into ingots.

Sometimes we may feel that our characters have been thoroughly cleaned and sanctified . . . but criticism stirs the pot again. Amazingly, we discover dross we didn't know we had. We react to the criticism in a manner that reveals our need for more stirring by the Spirit, and He uses the most unusual people to stir things up! No matter how many times the dross catches fire, more dross is always revealed.

Challenges, trials, even criticism "have come so that your faith—of greater worth than gold (*or lead*), which perishes even though refined by fire—may be proved genuine and may result in praise, glory and honor when Jesus Christ is revealed" (1 Peter 1:7, emphasis mine). We need the Holy Spirit to continue the refining process that makes us like Jesus, and sometimes He uses our critics to stir the pot.

Points to Ponder

1. Whose expectations are you trying to live up to? Your critic's? Your parent's? Your spouse's? Your church's? Your own expectations? Or God's expectations?
2. How can you best respond to a critic whose insecurities are a mirror image of your own?
3. Do you attract those who have a streak of rebellion? Are they critics of those who are unlike them? Are you?
4. How do you keep the wounds caused by criticism from pushing you toward being a person who wounds others? What steps might you take to heal your wounds?
5. Are you a control freak? How do you guard yourself against trying to control other people?

o o o o

CHAPTER
3

. . . .

Overlooking an Offense

"It is to one's glory to overlook an offense."
Proverbs 19:11

It is far better to step aside in small matters, so that we might stand
on the big ones. The bigness of a person can be judged by the size
of the thing upon which they take a stand. —E. Stanley Jones

An earnest young man made an appointment to see me. We had
never met, and I was anxious to know who he was and why he wanted
to talk to me. I learned that he had visited our church the previous
Sunday for the first time. Even with that limited experience, when he
came to my office he began to lambaste every aspect of the worship
service—from the welcome, to the music, to the message.

I let him jabber on while I formed a sharp rebuttal in mind. This
young fellow needed to be put in his place. Who was he to speak ill of
our church? We had a healthy, growing congregation. What right did he
have to criticize my preaching? I had been doing public speaking longer
than this whippersnapper had been alive. How could he sit in judgment
on us when he'd only attended one service? My anger was reaching a
boiling point. I was confident that I had come to the kingdom for such
a time as this. I could hardly wait for him to finish his critical diatribe
so I could let him have it—all in Christian love, of course!

But the Holy Spirit had other ideas. As I sat there listening, stew-
ing, and preparing my rebuttal, the Spirit gently reminded me of

Proverbs 15:1, "A gentle (soft, KJV) answer turns away wrath, but a harsh word stirs up anger." As that verse filtered through my mind and spirit I knew that I couldn't respond as I had planned. The bottled-up anger quickly dissipated. Instead, I said words to this effect: "You're probably right! We certainly can do things better than we're doing them now. I'm sure our greeters and ushers can be more accommodating. Our music's not perfect, and I can always improve in my speaking abilities. Thanks for bringing that to our attention."

Overlooking an offense may be a good response, or it may not be, depending on what the criticism is about and who offers it.

His reaction was quite remarkable, very much in keeping with the promise of the proverb. My soft response totally deflated and defused him. His animosity drained away. He didn't know what to say next. He'd been hoping for an argument but instead got a gentle answer. The end result was a nice conversation that turned to his spiritual needs instead of the church's deficiencies. Unfortunately, I never saw him again.

As I thought about it later, I recognized that my encounter with this young man provided a great lesson in how to overlook an offense. I also had to acknowledge that in similar situations I had not been as restrained or wise.

Overlooking an offense isn't always the best response. It depends on both the criticism and the critic. Since the young man's criticism was about rather minor issues, it didn't warrant a stiff defense. And since he had no standing or reputation in our church, his unkind comments could be taken as inconsequential.

However, if the criticism had targeted my integrity, it would probably have required a rebuttal. Or if the criticism had come from a respected colleague, it necessarily would have been taken more seriously. So overlooking an offense may be a good response, or it may not be, depending on what the criticism is about and who offers it.

The term translated *overlook* means *to go* or *pass over*. These words conjure up an image in my mind of a car going or passing over a chuckhole in the road. You certainly know there is a chuckhole and that you hit it, but you just keep going. You don't stop to examine the hole, or even repair the hole. You keep moving. The chuckhole may have some importance in the journey, but it's more important that you get to your destination. Criticism is like that. Sometimes you have to pass over it to get where the Lord wants you to go.

The devotional *The Word for You Today* uses a different illustration: "Have you ever watched water run off a duck's back? That's how you should treat unkind comments."[5] Shake criticism off. Every criticism doesn't need a response; it may need to be overlooked.

But I need to wave some flags of caution.

Don't Become Calloused

Calloses don't appear overnight. If I work in the yard (which I try to avoid doing), and I consistently use a shovel, a hoe, or push a lawn mower, my hands begin to develop calloses. They grow on the parts of my hands that get the most pressure. To begin with they can be quite sore, but over time they harden. If I stop my landscaping activity, the calloses soften and eventually disappear.

After lengthy periods of persistent criticism, calloses can develop on our hearts. We can become desensitized to even our mildest critics. Over time we can become hardened and unfeeling. This callousness should never be classified as overlooking an offense. Rather it reveals a heart that is unfeeling, numb, and untouched by words, good or bad.

Hardness of heart in one area of our lives affects all the other areas. We may have steeled ourselves against the snarls of our critics, but in so doing we may become hardened, not only to the words people say, but to the people themselves. Those for whom we should have compassion, we reject because of what they say.

Overlooking the offender is not the same as overlooking the offense. Having hardened our hearts against innuendo and verbal shots, we nevertheless cannot cut the people off who desperately need our love and ministry. Callousness about the criticism can develop into callousness toward the one who criticizes, and thus limits, if not destroys, any potential we may have to effectively minister to that person.

My Dad used to tell me, "A leader must have the hide of a rhinoceros, but maintain the heart of a child." I'm sure he never thought I would remember his words, but they have stuck with me because they are true. My defense against criticism can't grow into a callousness that impacts my life, my ministry, and my relationships with people.

Don't Be Touchy

Some who never become calloused face the opposite dilemma. They are hypersensitive. They take personally even the smallest criticism.

In World War II one of the oft-used weapons was mines. Aircraft placed the mines in the sea routes and harbors of the enemy with the goal of destroying their ships and boats. When an enemy ship hit a mine its explosive power blew a hole in the hull of the ship. There were various types of mines, one of which was the Daisy-chained mine. It was comprised of two moored, floating contact mines tethered together by a length of steel cable or chain. Each mine was situated approximately sixty feet away from its neighbor, and each floated several feet below the surface of the ocean. When the target ship hit the steel cable, the mines on either side were drawn down the side of the ship's hull and exploded on contact. It was almost impossible for the target ship to pass safely between the two individually moored mines.[6]

When I read about the Daisy-chained mines, this thought popped into my mind: "That reminds me of some people I know." A direct hit is not required for them to explode. If you just touch their "cable," the dark side of their personality manifests itself. Sometimes it's a part of their personality you didn't know existed.

Minor criticisms, even direct suggestions, can set them off. They go through life with their elbows out waiting for someone to bump into them. Their temper has a quick trigger, and their feelings get hurt easily. But you can't be an effective leader if you are hypersensitive.

When our kids were growing up and reached the dating age, we

. . . .

We don't want to be the kind of leader who easily takes offense, someone people have to tiptoe around.

. . . .

would often advise them, "Don't marry someone you have to walk on eggs around—where you have to wonder what kind of mood they're going to be in when they wake up in the morning. Marry someone who is even-tempered and lives on an even keel." To their credit, they took our advice.

We don't want to be the kind of leader who easily takes offense, someone people have to tiptoe around. When you are quick to be offended, it's extremely hard to overlook that offense.

Don't Repeat the Criticism

"He who covers over an offense promotes love, but whoever repeats the matter separates close friends" (Prov. 17:9).

When we rehearse the criticism in our minds or repeat it to other people, it means we haven't overlooked it. We haven't gotten past it. It's still doing its negative work in our spirit. We haven't passed over the chuckhole, but we're stuck in it.

Repeating the criticism embeds it like a barb in the mind and spirit. Like a fisherman setting the hook in a fish's mouth, repetition snags and hangs on to the criticism. The more we repeat it, either to ourselves or to others, the bigger it becomes to us. What started out as a small issue mushrooms into a major challenge.

If we go over and over it in our minds, we begin trying to find hidden meanings in the criticism. We think, *What did they mean by that? What motivated it? What was left unsaid that they probably wanted to say? What else are they unhappy about?* The imagination can concoct all sorts of scenarios, most of which have no roots in reality. Fresh interpretations distort what was said. Motives are impugned. Relationships are severed.

Stop the repetition!

Ask the Holy Spirit to expunge the criticism from your mind. Resist the temptation to tell somebody about it. Discipline your thinking so that it ceases to be at the forefront of your thought-life. Get out of the chuckhole and move on. Pass over the offense.

Bury the Criticism in Love

Have you ever noticed how parents and grandparents tend to overlook the shenanigans of their kids, especially young kids? Their impish antics provide amusement for the family, and consternation for those outside the family. Onlookers shake their heads in wonderment at what some parents let their kids get away with. These little hellions can terrorize the neighbor kids but their parents classify it as "cute." Or they'll say, "He's just like his dad!"

Outsiders wouldn't put up with the kids' misbehavior, and perhaps the parents shouldn't either. But the big difference between the outsiders and the parents is—the parents love their children more than the outsiders do. Love softens the edges of hardcore conduct. Certainly love sometimes prompts discipline, but it also makes allowances because of relationship.

I don't recall the source of the story, but years ago I read about two fathers. One of them had a son who was incorrigible. He was always in trouble. One issue would get settled and he would soon be embroiled in another. Numerous times he was an unwelcome guest at the local jail. But his father always came to his rescue, and helped him when he could.

As the two fathers talked about this wayward boy, the one father said to the other, "If that were my boy, I'd just give up on him." To which the second father said, "Well, if that were *your* boy, I'd give up on him too. But he's *my* boy, and I'll never give up on him or stop loving him."

The apostle Peter reminds us of that kind of tenacious love: "Above all, love each other deeply, because love covers over a multitude of sins" (1 Peter 4:8). Perhaps Peter was thinking about Proverbs 10:12: "Hatred stirs up dissension, but love covers over all wrongs." Proverbs 17:9 says much the same thing. "He who covers over an offense promotes love." These verses reveal a direct link between covering over an offense, even criticism, because of love.

The context of Peter's exhortation is important for us to note. He begins the paragraph with the overarching truth, "The end of all things is near" (1 Peter 4:7). That puts the offenses we may receive in proper perspective. Much criticism can be overlooked because life's too short to carry offenses around.

Then Peter talks about—

- Being clear minded and self-controlled, and how that attitude helps your prayer life
- Gifts of the Spirit that have come to us through grace
- Hospitality to one another
- Speaking the words of God
- Serving in God's strength

But in the middle of all these wonderful truths, he says, "Above all . . ." More than any of these other important matters, before doing anything else, "love each other deeply." Why? "Because love covers over a multitude of sins" (v. 8). That's why we can overlook the offense of criticism. We love the critic so much.

Remember, we aren't saying that every criticism should be overlooked and passed over. Some criticisms require a different response. But isn't it also true that we sometimes harbor criticism that could easily be overlooked because we don't love the critic as we should? Then it's time for *us* to have a spiritual EKG, because we may need a transfusion of divine love. That kind of love "keeps no record of wrongs" (1 Cor. 13:5).

I've done enough marital counseling to know that some husbands and wives have exceedingly long memories. A recent clash, upheaval, or argument triggers memories of what happened years ago. So one or the other will bolster their side of the story by dredging up old hurts, ancient offenses, and criticisms so old that they ought to be on *The Antiques Roadshow!* The couple may not be able to remember their spouse's birthday, but they can recall some flare-up they had twenty years ago. Counseling is a good place for them to be, but it offers little hope if they continue to keep score of their wrongs. Marriage isn't about winning, but loving. Their recollections and recounting of their spouse's past transgressions reveal that as a married couple they have a critical love deficit.

It happens in churches, too. A former board member can't remember his own phone number, but he can give you a blow-by-blow account of a dispute between him and the pastor in a board meeting years ago. His role in the argument is softened in his memory, but he can retell the pastor's harsh retorts word for word. Loving one another deeply isn't in the equation. Rather it's all about keeping a record of wrongs.

The psalmist asked, "If you, O LORD, kept a record of sins, O LORD, who could stand?" (Ps. 130:3). Good question. Easy answer: no one could stand. We can all look back and see a pattern of sin in our past. So the psalmist adds, "But with you there is forgiveness, therefore you are feared" (Ps. 130:4). The record has been cleared by Jesus' forgiveness.

If Jesus loved us enough to wipe the slate of our sin clean, how can we do less? When criticisms of little consequence begin to fester in our spirits, we possess the power of love that brings healing. That power enables us to overlook the criticism by burying it in love.

The Word tells us that God doesn't remember our sins once they are forgiven. Isn't that an amazing truth? "I, even I, am he who blots out your transgressions, for my own sake, and remembers your sins no more" (Isa. 43:25).

God is omniscient, all-knowing, so He doesn't forget anything. If He did, He wouldn't be omniscient. So when He says that He no longer remembers our sins, the meaning seems to be that He chooses not to remember. By a deliberate act of His will, He buries our transgressions in the vast expanse of His love. He knows where they are buried, but they will never be remembered or resurrected. He will never taunt us or bribe us with past sin. His choice to forget our sins means He will never use them against us.

We may not be able to forget past criticisms, but we can be like our heavenly Father and bury them in love, never to be brought up again.

Points to Ponder

1. Think of a time when you may have overreacted to a relatively minor criticism. How would you respond differently?
2. What types of criticism can be shaken off and overlooked?
3. In overlooking criticism, how can we keep from being hardhearted toward the critic?
4. Can you remember a time when you repeated a criticism and it created an even greater firestorm? What did you learn from this?
5. Ask God to give you a genuine love for the person criticizing you, a love that doesn't keep score.

o o o o

CHAPTER
4

. . . .

The Elijah Syndrome

"I have had enough, Lord . . . Take my life . . . I am the only one left. . . ."
1 Kings 19:4, 10

I had many, many times of self-pity . . . self-pity filled my mind many, many days. Always, however, I came back to one thing: God had chosen to keep me alive.—Don Piper

One of my more interesting, but exhausting, life-challenges was completing my doctoral studies while pastoring a growing church. It was during this intense personal season that I was forced to stretch my pastoral care muscles in a new direction: suicide. (Not my own!)

In a relatively short period of time I conducted several funerals for people who had taken their own lives. Some were from our congregation, but most were connected by family relationships or friendships with members of the church. One young lady had spent considerable time in our home—sharing meals with us, playing with our kids, and talking about her mental and emotional challenges. Her death by her own hand was very painful and personal for our family. I felt ill-equipped to effectively minister in such situations. Neither my education nor my experience provided adequate preparation for ministering to the bereaved families or conducting a funeral that would provide much-needed comfort.

My doctoral work converged with the reality of my pastoral in-adequacies in dealing with the theological, biblical, and practical aspects of suicide. So when confronted with my dissertation proposal, I presented a brief on the unlikely subject, "How the Church Ministers to the Suicidal and their Survivor Victims." To my amazement and a trace of chagrin, it was approved.

I soon realized I was in serious trouble! Nothing in my background or education had prepared me to write on such a subject. Psychology and counseling were not my main interests. I was a churchman and a pastor, and not a very good counselor. But now I was on a path that required me to prepare a scholarly work on a topic about which my knowledge was minimal. Nevertheless the study-experience was eye-opening. My learning curve about this unpleasant issue took a sharp spike. Eventually the dissertation was completed and affirmed, and I graduated.

Part of the biblical research included a study of those characters in Scripture who committed suicide, as well as those who were tempted to do so. That latter group included Elijah, the Old Testament prophet. I concluded that the suicidal impulse was not exclusive to him but that every person, including a professed Christian, can question whether life is worth living. That is not to say that they *should* feel that way, but that a grim outlook on life, negative personal circumstances, and the insidious inroads of the Destroyer can plant self-destructive thoughts in the mind. We all can be susceptible.

Interestingly Elijah's suicidal impulse was expressed through prayer. "'I have had enough, LORD,' he said. 'Take my life . . . I am the only one left.'" (1 Kings 19:4, 10). He wanted to die, but didn't want to kill himself. He wanted God to do it for him! This is an amazing example of why we can be thankful that God doesn't always give us a positive answer to our prayers. Elijah's prayer was self-serving and contrary to God's will, and sometimes ours are as well.

How had this mighty prophet sunk so low in spirit? How could this remarkable man of God, who called fire down from heaven (1 Kings 18), have plunged into such depression? His dive into despair seemed to be precipitated by a threat from a woman, Queen Jezebel. She said, "May the gods deal with me, be it ever so severely, if by this time tomorrow I do not make your life like that of one of them [*the prophets of Baal killed by Elijah*]" (1 Kings 19:2, emphasis mine). In other words, "Elijah, I'm going kill you to get revenge for your slaughter of Baal's prophets!"

Elijah had good reason to be concerned, because Jezebel was far more dangerous and murderous than her husband, King Ahab. In fact she was the motivator behind some of his most evil acts. "There was never a man like Ahab, who sold himself to do evil in the eyes of the LORD, *urged on by Jezebel his wife*" (1 Kings 21:25, emphasis mine). She thought nothing of conspiring to kill Naboth in order to secure his vineyard for Ahab (1 Kings 21). She launched a campaign to annihilate all the prophets of the Lord who challenged her life-long worship of Baal. Her father, Ethbaal, was king of the Sidonians (1 Kings 16:31). His name meant *Baal's man*. So in her upbringing Jezebel had known nothing but Baal worship. Now as an adult she fed 850 prophets of Baal and Asherah at her table (1 Kings 18:19), while continuing her pogrom against the Lord's prophets (1 Kings 18:4, 13).

So Elijah's confrontation and destruction of the prophets of Baal and Asherah on Mount Carmel elicited her vow of revenge. She determined to kill Elijah, so he "was afraid and ran for his life" (1 Kings 19:3). His ambiguity about dying was obvious. Jezebel was ready and willing to answer his prayer, "Let me die." She would have been delighted to end his life. Instead, he hightailed it, getting as far away from her as he could . . . then he asked God to kill him. Despite the seriousness of the story, you have to see the humor in it.

Syndrome and Susceptibility

Let's admit that there's a significant difference between a threat on someone's life and criticism of that person's leadership. One can be deadly, while the other is not. As sharp, cutting, and persistent as the criticism may be, it doesn't rise to the level of a death threat. However, the way Elijah responded to the threat isn't unlike how we may respond to criticism. I call his response The Elijah Syndrome.

A syndrome is defined as "a recognizable pattern of signs, symptoms, and/or behaviors."[7] When people criticize us, we are susceptible to the same pattern of negative behavior that Elijah had—psychological and emotional letdowns, physical exhaustion, isolation, misperceptions, and self-pity. We may not go so far as to ask God to let us die, but we certainly can hit bottom.

Look Out for Letdowns

Elijah's confrontation with the prophets of Baal on Mount Carmel is well chronicled in 1 Kings 18. We won't rehearse it here. But Elijah's brief prayer is worth noting: "O LORD, God of Abraham, Isaac and Israel, let it be known today that you are God in Israel and that I am

. . . .

We can be especially susceptible to spiritual letdowns after a great victory.

. . . .

your servant and have done all these things at your command. Answer me, O LORD, answer me, so these people will know that you, O LORD, are God, and that you are turning their hearts back again" (1 Kings 18:36–37). And the Lord answered with fire! What a victory. What a vindication of God's sovereignty, and validation of the prophet's word.

But victories take their toll—before, during, and after the win. We can be especially susceptible to spiritual letdowns after a great victory. After we've reached a worthy goal, what then? Often, at these low points, the Enemy prompts critics to fire their sharpest arrows. Perhaps when we've climbed the mountain of success, we feel invincible. Like David we say, "By thee I have run through a troop; and by my God have I leaped over a wall" (Ps. 18:29, KJV). Everything seems possible! We aren't prepared for the emotional, psychological, and physical letdown that often occurs after the victory, and in those valleys of the soul any criticism directed at us personally or at the victory just realized can be overwhelming.

We can't live on the mountain of accomplishment forever, any more than Peter, James, and John could stay on the Mount of Transfiguration. They had to come down the mountain to face life's realities, and so do we. Everyone has letdowns. Criticism may come when we're on the mountain or when we're experiencing our biggest letdown. In either case we won't be cowed by negative words. The God who took us to the pinnacle of success will guard us when we experience a normal letdown.

Rebound from Exhaustion

Have you noticed that criticism seems to cut a wider swath in our hearts when we're weary? Elijah was exhausted. Not only had he been through an intense spiritual battle, but afterwards he engaged in faith-filled prayer that brought rain. We don't know how long he prayed, but it was sufficiently long that he was able to ask his servant seven times to go look toward the sea. Eventually the servant saw "a cloud as small as a man's hand . . . rising from the sea" (1 Kings 18:44). Such intercession is hard work. It can be physically exhausting.

In addition, Elijah told Ahab to hitch up the chariots and try to beat the rainstorm. Then the power of the Lord came on Elijah, and he ran ahead of Ahab's chariot from Carmel to Jezreel, a distance of about sixteen miles.[8] I don't know if Ahab's horses walked, trotted, or galloped, but the prophet was ahead of them all the way.

Then upon hearing the threat from Jezebel, Elijah went to Beersheba, a distance of at least eighty miles, and from there he made a trek—a day's journey—into the desert. In that desolate place he prayed his suicidal prayer, and then fell asleep. No wonder! Despite supernatural help, Elijah had traveled about one hundred miles, having run sixteen miles of that trip. This was on top of his spiritual battle on Carmel and his extensive prayer-time.

Leadership can be exhausting! A single mom who works full-time comes home to fix dinner, clean house, do laundry, finally go to bed, and then get up the next morning to do it all over again. Exhausting! A start-up business doesn't have the cash flow to hire "help," so the owner and his family members work long hours to build financial success. Exhausting! The spiritual burden pastors carry for their congregations motivates them to devote themselves to meet overwhelming needs. Exhausting!

Without adequate self-care, exhausted leaders can be susceptible to temptation, depression, and anger. Criticism can push them over the edge. It cuts them more deeply when they are tired. They need to follow Elijah's example and get some much-needed sleep. I heard a highly respected leader say, "One of the most spiritual things you can do sometimes is to take a nap!" Over the years I've enjoyed developing my spirituality in this way! If we don't take care of ourselves, no one else will. But the good news is that we can rebound from our weariness. We may not have angels to take care of us like Elijah did, but we can take steps to ensure we stay rested.

Avoid Isolation

Criticism born alone seems to have sharper edges. Sharing it with those we trust seems to soften those edges.

When Elijah left Beersheba to go into the desert, he left his servant behind. At his lowest moment, when he most needed someone to be with him, he was alone. He deliberately isolated himself. He may just have been hiding from Jezebel. Maybe he thought God would answer his prayer and wanted a geographical no man's land to be his final resting place. Nonetheless his isolation was complete.

When our critics are hounding us, we usually have no place to hide. We can't run to the desert like Elijah did. But we can withdraw emotionally, using our withdrawal as a shield. It keeps people at a distance from us and may indeed protect us from more criticism. But it also repels those closest to us, those who love us the most. So through self-protection we may gain a sense of security but lose the openness to people who have so much to contribute to our lives. Such isolation is counterproductive.

It's instructive that one of the first assignments God gave Elijah after his withdrawal was to anoint Elisha as his successor. But the succession didn't take place immediately. The Scriptures are unclear what span of time elapsed between Elijah anointing Elisha and his miraculous ascent into heaven, but it seems to have been several years. Perhaps Elisha was meant to be not only his successor, but his companion. Wouldn't it be interesting to know the conversations that took place between them? Every Elijah needs an Elisha to walk with him through the good times and the bad. Isolation offers no comfort when we're assailed from every side.

When we're discouraged or depressed, unwelcome criticism can seem like a mountain looming over us when in reality it's just a non-threatening molehill.

Refocus Perceptions

When we're discouraged or depressed, unwelcome criticism can seem like a mountain looming over us when in reality it's just a non-threatening molehill. During spiritual lows our perceptions of what is true can be skewed, and our minds conjure up worse-case scenarios. Our imaginations get stuck in negative grooves that replay all sorts of options that never come to pass. Without the Lord's help and the encouragement of good friends, we can begin to believe that our misperceptions are reality.

Elijah had lost perspective. As great as this man of God was, his focus was blurry. He needed to refocus, and understand what was true. Here are some of his misperceptions:

- He imagined that he was the only one left serving God. Perhaps his isolation contributed to this perception. The Lord reminded him, "I reserve seven thousand in Israel—all whose knees have not bowed down to Baal and all whose mouths have not kissed him" (1 Kings 19:18).
- He affirmed that the Israelites as a nation had been putting God's prophets to death. But it was really only Jezebel who initiated this action. She would have had followers who did her bidding, but she was the one behind this killing of the prophets. Elijah thought all the people of Israel were behind this terrible deed.
- He assumed his death at Jezebel's hand was inevitable. But the Lord still had a work for him to do, including the anointing of his successor.

When low tides come, whether through criticism or other challenges, our perceptions and/or misperceptions require that we refocus.
That's why it's wise not to respond immediately to criticism when
you're discouraged. Our responses will be tainted by our false view
of things.

While writing this chapter, my devotional discipline has been to
read five chapters of the Psalms each day for thirty days. This con-
centrated re-reading has reminded me that King David often talked
about his enemies. He always seemed to be surrounded by people who
wanted the worst for him. Some, like King Saul, wanted to take his
life. Others wounded him with cutting words. "Not a word from their
mouth can be trusted; their heart is filled with destruction. Their throat
is an open grave; with their tongue they speak deceit. Declare them
guilty, O God" (Ps. 5:9–10)! In describing his foes, David occasionally
lapses into hyperbole, or perhaps poetic license.

But he doesn't stop there. He also affirms the greatness of God
and God's infinite capacity to deliver. "Praise be to the LORD, for he has
heard my cry for mercy. The LORD is my strength and my shield; my
heart trusts in him, and I am helped" (Ps. 28:6).

David had the capacity to refocus. He didn't deny that he had enemies, but he shifted his focus from them to the God he served by offering praise to God. What a powerful example of perception-correction.

Guard Against Self-Pity

In Elijah's whining about how zealous he had been for the Lord,
complaining about being the only one left, and expressing his desire
to die, you can quickly detect the unmistakable sound of self-pity. If
he had said, "Woe is me," we wouldn't have been surprised.

In college I was part of a number of different gospel teams.
During the summer we sang and preached our way around the Northwest. When you travel with others non-stop for a few months, even if
they're good friends you get to know their foibles and idiosyncrasies
pretty well.

One of our team members was nearly always positive and happy,
but when he wasn't, everyone knew it. When he was in a funk, he

majored in self-pity, and he wasn't quiet about it either. He would verbalize his complaints—his feelings were hurt, he wasn't appreciated, he worked harder than anyone else.

The rest of us quickly recognized his occasional tendency toward self-pity, and we did what normal college students would do. We teased him! We accused him of having taken too many "martyr pills." The teasing usually helped get him out of the doldrums and before long he was his happy self again. Of course we all knew about martyr pills because at different times we had all taken our share of them, too.

At the risk of sounding irreverent, we could say that Elijah had taken his martyr pills. We recognize it because, like the gospel team members, we've done it too; we've felt sorry for ourselves. Few things can cause us to fall headlong into self-pity faster than criticism. We don't feel appreciated. Others are not the recipients of harsh words like we are. Our hurt feelings exacerbate the criticism beyond its clear meaning. No one else might notice it, but we're being victimized, or so we think.

. . . .

Criticism can reveal the cracks in our character, and self-pity can unveil the hold self has on us.

. . . .

So does self-pity create a sense of victimization, or does a victim fall into self-pity, or both? I honestly don't know the answer to that. I do know that victims feel like they have little or no control over their lives. For instance, they can't control what others say about them. They struggle to take responsibility for their decisions. What happens to them is always someone else's fault. (Elijah blamed Jezebel for his dilemma.) Their perspective is narrow and self-centered. No wonder they feel sorry for themselves!

Self-pity is rooted in the *self*. It's all about us. The world revolves around us. Everyone else should cater to our desires and feelings.

What a contrast to the apostle Paul's perspective. When he met with the Ephesian elders for the last time, he said, "In every city the Holy Spirit warns me that prison and hardships are facing me"

(Acts 20:23). Prisons and hardships are much worse than any criticism we might face, but Paul didn't complain nor did he wallow in self-pity. His response? "None of these things move me, neither count I my life dear unto myself" (Acts 20:24, KJV).

When people fire criticism at us, we are too easily moved. Our lives are too dear to us. Self is still too dominant. Even when the negative words are unjust and unkind, self can be aroused and inflamed. Criticism can reveal the cracks in our character, and self-pity can unveil the hold self has on us. These revelations remind us that we still need to make progress in our spiritual development. They can spur us on to self-denial and a crucified life.

Death of a Dream

When people criticize us, we may not pray Elijah's prayer, "Take my life." However, verbal arrows can cause the death of a dream God has planted in our hearts. Let me give you an example from my pastoral world.

> Eric Reed, of *Leadership Journal,* writes that 19,200 pastors annually are required to leave the ministry (*Leadership Journal,* January, 2006). Most leave the ministry due to tension and stress, but money, depression, leadership confusion, and lack of a clear strategy for moving their church forward also play a role.[9]

That's hard for me to grasp: 19,200 pastors annually, 1,600 monthly, 53 daily. These are ministers who at one time sensed God's call on their lives, prepared themselves through education and experience, and were "hands on" in ministry. It leaves me wondering how much of the tension, stress, and depression was caused by criticism—words designed to tear down. While we will never be able to know all the causes, we know that their departure from vocational ministry brought about the death of a dream.

Some dreams deserve to die. They were conjured up out of our own imaginations. God didn't inspire them. But other dreams were prompted by Him, and it's a tragedy to to allow criticism to kill those dreams. None of us want our epitaphs to be, "What might have been!" We want God's dream to live brightly, to be fulfilled in His time, and to allow us to participate in its completion.

Points to Ponder

1. Do you identify with Elijah in his post-Carmel experience? If so, in what areas do you identify with him?
2. When criticized, do you tend to withdraw from people or seek them out? Why do you think you react as you do?
3. Can you remember a time when you had a letdown after a big event? How did you deal with it in a positive way?
4. What feelings do you have when you are totally exhausted? What activities do you engage in to recharge?
5. Do you take "martyr pills"? When? Why? What areas of self-pity do you need to conquer with the Lord's help?

o o o o

CHAPTER
5

· ·

The Hezekiah Model

"You intended to harm me, but God intended it for good. . . ."
Genesis 50:20

Ever since that third day, whatever bad news may enter your life has no power to separate you from God.—John Ortberg

I hate receiving anonymous correspondence, whether it's a letter in the mail, a response card from the pew rack, or a connection card from the church bulletin. When it's unsigned, it becomes a red flag that warns: "Read at your own risk."

I know that I should have a more positive attitude toward the nameless authors who pen these missives, but I don't. Having read too many of them already, my experience tells me they seldom are complimentary. Hence my negative attitude.

As a minister I've chatted with pastoral colleagues about how they handle these messages of unknown origin. Many of them have responded, "I don't read them. I immediately throw them in the trash." When *the trash* is translated into theological jargon it's like saying they were cast into *outer darkness*. To my carnal nature *outer darkness* sounds like a good place, not only for the correspondence, but for the anonymous writers as well. But of course I'm much too spiritual to say so.

Nevertheless, once or twice I decided to follow the example of those wise pastors who offered the sage advice to disregard and discard unsigned correspondence. So the next time an anonymous letter or card arrived, I promptly deposited it in my wastebasket—unread. That should have been the end of it, but my active curiosity shifted into overdrive. While proceeding with other work, my mind kept wandering from the task at hand. "I wonder who's upset now. Maybe So-and-So is fussing again. I'd sure like to know what they said. Maybe I could recognize the handwriting, and figure out who wrote it." I'm far, far too curious to leave anonymous letters in the wastebasket.

So before long I would be grubbing about through the discarded contents in the trash trying to find the one piece of paper that had no signature. When I found it and read the criticism it contained, I wished I had left it in the trash. It confirmed my dislike for such communications. Most of the time they were less than encouraging; often they were sharp and unkind, and sometimes hurtful and demeaning. That's why I resisted reading them in the first place.

I confess that I don't have much respect for anonymous writers. It seems obvious that they don't have the gumption to take responsibility for their assertions; they won't stand up for what they believe. Perhaps they don't have the guts to challenge the leader face to face. In many cases, chronic complainers use the unsigned note to give vent to their persistent whining. Those pastors who advocated for *the trash* acknowledge that whiners exist, but they won't give them a written hearing for their negativity. I guess I'm not as smart as they are!

Is It True?

After receiving an anonymous note, there have been times when I've asked myself, *Is there any truth in what's being said? Even though it's said in a hurtful way, is there a kernel of truth in it? Is it something I need to hear?* Not always, but sometimes, the critic put a finger on a weakness, a flaw, or poor judgment.

Could it be that the reason some criticism, whether written or verbal, hurts so much is because it's true? Am I able to face the issues my critics raise, especially when it's personal?

Criticism automatically arouses defense mechanisms. Rebuttals instantly rise in our minds. We arm ourselves for verbal combat even

. . . .

If you're ever in doubt about whether the criticism is justified, ask trusted friends and colleagues for their perspective.

. . . .

when we don't know who our critics are. We justify ourselves, and rationalize our behavior or decisions. We are too quick to put on our armor, and too ready for combat.

If you're ever in doubt about whether the criticism is justified, ask trusted friends and colleagues for their perspective. More than once I took issues raised by anonymous writers to my pastoral staff meetings. My wise and honest coworkers were not hesitant about either discarding the criticism or dealing with its truth. Their collective wisdom was far greater than mine alone, and I profited by their sanctified insights.

In other instances I would take the anonymous letter, and following King Hezekiah's example, I spread it out before the Lord and from my knees asked Him, "Is there truth in this letter that I need to hear and acknowledge?"

Hezekiah was the twelfth king of Judah. His reign was one of spiritual reform. The Scripture says of him, "Hezekiah trusted in the Lord, the God of Israel. There was no one like him among all the kings of Judah, either before him or after him . . . and the Lord was with him; he was successful in whatever he undertook" (2 Kings 18:5–7). However, he rebelled against the king of Assyria, which placed him and his kingdom in jeopardy.

Twice the king of Assyria threatened Hezekiah, first with a verbal threat and then a written threat. Between the two, Sennacherib withdrew his troops to fight against the Egyptians. But before his withdrawal he sent the written message to Judah's king. "Hezekiah received the letter from the messengers and read it. Then he went up to the temple of the Lord and spread it out before the Lord. And Hezekiah prayed to the Lord" (2 Kings 19:14–15).

We are not under threat of an invasion by a hostile enemy. Coping with criticism is far less perilous than a siege of Jerusalem. Discovering the truth hidden in an anonymous correspondence can't be compared to the ominous war clouds that hung over Judah. But we can learn from Hezekiah's model. Under threat he immediately went to the temple for prayer. He spread out the blasphemous words of Sennacherib before the Lord, and appealed for God's help.

When we read Hezekiah's prayer, it's evident that he was less concerned about the destruction of Jerusalem than he was about the affront to his God. He prayed, "Listen to the words Sennacherib has sent to insult the living God" (2 Kings 19:16). Sennacherib's field commander had the audacity to say, "The LORD himself told me to march against this country and destroy it" (2 Kings 18:25). Sennacherib himself had compared the God of Israel with the gods of the other nations he had conquered, gods unable to come to their aid. Hezekiah was appalled by the comparison and appealed for deliverance "so that all kingdoms on earth may know that you alone, O LORD, are God" (2 Kings 19:19).

Whether or not we have a letter to spread out before the Lord, we can have a Hezekiah-spirit. We can pray. We can be less concerned about the hurts criticism has inflicted on us. God's reputation is more important than our own. The criticism may in fact be aimed at Him, and we can pray that His name will be vindicated.

Who's the Messenger?

The fact that I don't like anonymous messengers doesn't mean I can ignore the message when it contains the truth.

A recurring theme of the Old Testament is the impassioned condemnation by the prophets of Israel's idolatry, shameful backsliding, and hardheartedness. They foretold impending judgment. They pled for national repentance. But in most cases the people didn't respond. They ignored the message or pressured the prophet to change it.

"They say to the seers, 'See no more visions!' and to the prophets, 'Give us no more visions of what is right! Tell us pleasant things, prophesy illusions'" (Isa. 30:10). "Speak unto us smooth things, prophesy deceits" (Isa. 30:10, KJV). In other words, tell us what we want to hear.

When the prophets continued to declare God's message, the people not only rejected the message, they attacked the messenger. The prophets were imprisoned, tortured, or killed because of their messages. Israel's attitude was—if you don't like the message, attack the messenger.

This extreme example reminds us that we need to make a distinction between the message and the messenger, between the criticism and the critic. The prophets were godly men and women who delivered unpopular messages. The critic may not be godly, may have evil intent, and may desire to hurt. In such cases we tend to attack the critic in order to invalidate the criticism. But what if the Lord is using an unlikely messenger to tell us something we need to hear?

. . . .

The message is always more important than the messenger, even when that person's criticism is meant to bring harm.

. . . .

God used a money-grubbing prophet, Balaam, to prophesy blessing over Israel (Num. 22–24). The high priest, Caiaphas, was a rascal, but he accurately prophesied that Jesus would die for the Jewish nation (John 11:49–52). God sometimes chooses the most unlikely people to get His message across. After all, He chose some of us.

Could God use an unworthy, even ornery, person to deliver an unwanted but needed message to us? Could God's message to us actually be wrapped in criticism? Could God take sharp and hurtful words from a critic with wrong motivation to speak truth to us? Yes, yes, and yes! The message is always more important than the messenger, even when that person's criticism is meant to bring harm.

With most criticism there is little if any truth to be found. My pastor friends are probably right in not reading anonymous criticisms. But occasionally a seed of truth is discovered, and we dare not ignore it simply because it was delivered with words intended to wound by someone we count as unworthy.

Constructive Criticism?

What about constructive criticism? The phrase itself—*constructive criticism*—is an oxymoron. By its very nature criticism isn't intended to be constructive. Usually when someone offers what they call constructive criticism, it still has a sharp bite to it, and you sense their enjoyment in delivering it.

Rather than constructive criticism, the Bible (KJV) uses the word *correction*; the NIV often translates it as *instruction*.[10] The Greek verb means "to train up a child." In the King James Version, this verb is often translated as *chasten* to denote the aspect of loving discipline. It is used in Hebrews to remind us that "the Lord disciplines (chastens) those he loves (Heb. 12:6).

So correction is different from criticism. Correction is not prompted by animus or ill will, but is motivated by love. It seeks the highest and the best for the one receiving the correction whereas criticism is bent on cutting down and hurting.

A wonderful lady in one of our pastorates was a study in contrasts. She was kind but outspoken, warm but forceful, caring but cantankerous. When she should have been silent, she spoke. When she should have spoken, she did—again, and again, and again.

For some reason she liked and respected me as her pastor. Nevertheless she seemed to think it was her responsibility to help me toe the line. If she thought I misspoke during the message, or said something that was not quite true to the Word, she would confront me after the service and pressure me to admit my error. She wasn't unkind about it, but neither would she let me off the hook.

After service I would be walking to my office in another building, and I would hear the click, click, click of high heels moving quickly across the parking lot, accompanied by a feminine voice, "Pastor! Pastor!" I always knew who it was. She wouldn't let me get away without airing her feelings.

I could have taken umbrage at this persistent lady. I could have viewed her as a pest (sometimes I did). I could have pulled rank on her and dismissed her assertions. But I knew her heart. She loved me as her pastor, and she cared enough to confront me with what she thought were important points. Nine times out of ten she was right. I accepted it as correction that I needed. "Whoever heeds correction gains understanding" (Prov. 15:32). I also found that accepting the correction dashed whatever pride I might have had; it humbled me.

Sometimes God sends others to humble us, even through correction, because we have failed to humble ourselves under His mighty hand.

In contrast, criticism doesn't bear the fruit of humility. It's demeaning. It can cause us to think less of ourselves than God does. It creates an atmosphere where truth is clouded and distortions have clarity. It isn't intended for our good, but seeks to harm us.

. . . .

We can look for the kernel of truth in the criticism and use it to improve ourselves.

. . . .

Use the Abuse

So how do we handle critical and abusive words? Of course we can't answer those whose written criticism is unsigned. Some criticism is so absurd that it needs no answer. And it's simply unwise to try to answer every abusive blast that comes our way.

But we can do this: We can look for the kernel of truth in the criticism and use it to improve ourselves. We can allow God to turn to our benefit what others mean to harm us.

I accepted the pastorate of a church with the understanding that some changes would need to be made. In particular the church board and I had agreed in advance on a substantive change that would greatly enhance the effectiveness of my leadership. But sometimes good people say they want change, yet when it comes down to actually doing it, they have a difficult time.

Based on my understanding of our agreement and the board's commitment, I proposed the change to the congregation shortly after I became the pastor. It was soundly defeated, and the chief cause for its demise was a lack of support from the board.

A week or so later, a board member invited me for lunch. I had developed a good relationship with him during the pastoral search process. I trusted him. But over lunch he leveled his verbal howitzers at me for bringing the issue to the congregation at all. His direct and articulate criticism ruined my lunch! I left the restaurant reeling emotionally. I understood the psalmist's words, "If an enemy were insulting me, I could endure it; if a foe were raising himself against me, I could hide from him. But it is you, a man like myself, my companion, my close friend" (Ps. 55:12–13). The sharp manner in which he delivered the criticism hurt more than what he said. In many ways it redefined our relationship. It took me awhile to recover from his blasts.

In various roles of leadership, I've often reflected on what I could learn from this unexpected conversation. Among other questions, I asked myself, "Did I miss God's timing in presenting a significant change to the church membership?" In other words, was my friend right? I came to the conclusion that he was. I misread the commitment of the board to support the proposal. I had not pastored there long enough for people to trust my leadership to the extent that they would follow my recommended changes. As a deliberate decision-maker, I had not been deliberate enough.

That was a powerful, positive lesson for me to learn. The lesson was taught very painfully. It could have been delivered in a much more encouraging manner. But it helped me as a leader to always consider the timing of change before proposing it. So even though this board member had slapped me down verbally, the long-term result was to help me be a better decision-maker.

Isn't it just like the Lord to turn bad things, even criticism, into good things that ultimately enrich our lives? We see this divine practice over and over in the Scripture:

- God transformed Job's losses into twice what he had before.
- Out of Sarah's barrenness came the promised son, Isaac.
- Betrayal by Joseph's brothers produced provision that preserved the family from which the Messiah would come.
- Pharoah's decree to kill the Hebrew baby boys resulted in Moses being raised and educated as royalty.
- Paul's arrest and imprisonment gave him opportunity to witness to the Sanhedrin, Felix and his wife, Drusilla, Porcius Festus, King Agrippa, and Bernice.

God can and does turn evil into good. We often quote Romans 8:28, "In all things God works for the good of those who love him, who have been called according to his purpose." But such a quote omits a key part of the verse. The entire verse has more meaning when we see how it begins, "*And we know* that in all things God works for the good of those who love him . . ."

We know . . .

We know that unjust criticism can be turned to our good.
We know that hurtful words can develop compassion.
We know that how we deal with slander can change our reputation for the better in the end.
We know that our providential God sees the bigger picture, but has not forgotten us.
We know that we can trust God even when we are under attack.

And Jesus knows . . .

He knows what it is to be reviled.
He knows about verbal and physical abuse.
He knows about betrayal.
He knows about friends forsaking Him, but . . .
He knows the third day is coming.

In the crucible of suffering were the seeds of resurrection. From the broken body striped with lashes, healing is still available. His precious blood is a stream of salvation, liquid grace, available for all. The first day seemed like the end, but the third day was a new beginning.

Criticism is never final. God gets the last word.

Points to Ponder

1. The last time you were criticized and under attack, how did you respond? Would you have done anything differently? If so, what?
2. Have you been able to distinguish between criticism and correction? If so, what made the difference? If not, why not?
3. Think back to a time when God turned something bad into something good in your life. Thank Him for doing that. What did you learn about Him in the process? What did you learn about yourself?

4. Have you ever ignored truth in a criticism because you didn't like the messenger? What fallout, if any, developed from ignoring that truth?

5. Give thanks to Jesus for understanding what you are going through because He has gone through it too.

o o o o

CHAPTER
6

· · · · · · · · · · · · · · · · · · · ·
The Jesus Way

"Love your enemies, do good to those who hate you, bless those who curse you,
pray for those who mistreat you."
Luke 6:27–28

"Plain and simple: Mean people need Jesus. They will be in my prayers tonight . . . 1 Peter 2:1–25."—Carrie Underwood

In a much-ballyhooed television remake of *The Sound of Music*, singer Carrie Underwood starred as the central character, Maria von Trapp. This famous Rodgers & Hammerstein musical first debuted on Broadway in 1959. Later in 1965 it was made into a movie starring Julie Andrews. At the Academy Awards ceremony it won the Oscar for Best Picture. Though Julie Andrews was runner-up for Best Actress in a Leading Role, her portrayal of Maria von Trapp elevated her to iconic status.

Carrie Underwood was not so fortunate. In spite of the fact that she faced the challenge of performing live on NBC—no retakes allowed—the critics and many viewers panned both her acting and singing. "Not only was she bashed for a less-than-perfect portrayal of Julie Andrews' Maria von Trapp character from the general public, but also from stars from the original film."[11] That had to hurt.

Underwood responded to the sharp criticism by tweeting: "Plain and simple: Mean people need Jesus. They will be in my prayers tonight . . . 1 Peter 2:1–25."[12] Not every actress would have responded so kindly.

It seemed unusual to me that she would cite 1 Peter, so I looked it up. Verses 1–25 constitute the entire second chapter, and certainly all of the verses do not apply to her or her critics. While we don't know the thought processes that prompted Underwood to include the whole chapter in her tweet, some of the verses that seem to have a bearing are:

- "Therefore, rid yourselves of all malice and all deceit, hypocrisy, envy and slander of every kind" (v. 1).
- "Show proper respect to everyone" (v. 17).
- "But if you suffer for doing good and you endure it, this is commendable before God" (v. 20).
- "When they hurled their insults at him [Jesus], he did not retaliate; when he suffered he made no threats" (v. 23).

Whatever Underwood's intent, she got one thing absolutely right: Praying for our critics is a proper Christ-like response to harsh words. By praying for those who were unkind and mean she was following Jesus' instructions. "Love your enemies, do good to those who hate you, bless those who curse you, pray for those who mistreat you" (Luke 6:27–28).

Pray. Bless. Do good. Love. This is the Jesus way.

Pray

Praying is not what we feel like doing when we're being flayed by our detractors. Our defense mechanisms begin working overtime. Our emotions are muddled. Our minds concoct clever and cutting retorts. Our lower natures conjure ways and means to get back at our critics. Prayer isn't usually our first response. It's often the last resort.

But prayer is an active and appropriate response to criticism. It's a spiritual activity we can control. We can't control the critics or what they say. We could try to use our leadership positions to intimidate them. We could cow them into submission with an outpouring of anger. We could outtalk them with persuasive and irrefutable arguments. But those attempts at control would be short-lived and prove to be counterproductive.

• •

Prayer isn't about controlling those who criticize us or even about answering them. Prayer is an act of obedience.

• •

In contrast, prayer isn't about controlling those who criticize us or even about answering them. Prayer is an act of obedience. It follows the example of Jesus, as well as many other godly leaders, who have shown us how and when to pray.

- Jesus from the cross: "Father, forgive them, for they do not know what they are doing" (Luke 23:34).
- Nehemiah when threatened by Sanballat and Tobiah: "But we prayed to our God and posted a guard day and night to meet this threat" (Neh. 4:9).
- Stephen at his martyrdom: "Lord, do not hold this sin against them" (Acts 7:60).
- Moses, after Miriam and Aaron challenged his leadership and Miriam became leprous: "O God, please heal her" (Num. 12:13)!

When we are under verbal fire, prayer should be one of our first responses.

When We Pray the Wrong Prayers

If our prayers go unanswered, it could be that we are praying the wrong prayers—prayers not in the will of God.

Prayers of Vengeance

I heard one fellow ask God to, "Shake 'em over hell on a rotten stick!" While that's somewhat humorous, he was really asking God to do what he would like to do. He was attempting to enlist God to take his side in the battle. But what does God do if the person we are praying vengeance on is also a believer? Does God take our side against that person?

God is on the side of righteousness, grace, forgiveness, and justice. Our prayers need to ensure, not that God is on our side, but that we are on His.

We like to remind God (as if He had forgotten and needed reminding) that His Word says, "'It is mine to avenge; I will repay,' says the Lord" (Rom. 12:19). But the same passage says, "Do not repay anyone evil for evil. . . . Do not take revenge" (Rom. 12:17, 19). So when we pray for God's vengeance, we usurp His rightful place as the avenger. No wonder He doesn't answer our prayers!

Prayers Against Our Critics

Can we rightfully pray *against* those who criticize us? Leaders being criticized have said to me, "I'm under attack right now, but I am praying against my critics." Is that prayer in the will of God?

Without splitting hairs it seems to me that we must make a distinction between praying against the criticism and praying against the critic. We are certainly justified in praying that God will annul, bring to naught, and blunt untrue, unjust, and hateful criticism. The armor of God outlined in Ephesians 6 defends us, but prayer is an offensive weapon that is to be used in spiritual conflict.

However, praying against the critic is out of bounds. Ephesians 6 also tells us that "our struggle is not against flesh and blood, but against rulers, against the authorities, against the powers of this dark world and against the spiritual forces of evil in the heavenly realms" (Eph. 6:12). So people, even our critics, are not really the enemy we should pray against. In fact we should pray *for* such people, not against them.

Later in this chapter we will consider Jesus' exhortation to "bless those who curse you." The word *curse* means "to pray against, to wish evil against a person . . . uttered out of malevolence."[13] Blessing the critics and cursing or praying against them is a contradiction. When we pray, we want to be sure our petitions are those the Lord would delight in answering.

When We Pray the Right Prayers

When we do pray the right prayers, it gives us amazing confidence (1 John 5:14–15). We pray with faith and assurance. It produces powerful, positive results.

Prayer Changes Attitudes

As a pastor-leader I made an important decision regarding our approach to adult discipleship in the church. As with any significant decision, it wasn't met with overwhelming accolades. One man in particular took umbrage at it, feeling that it was intended to impinge on the best exercise of his gifts. Indeed he was gifted and held several key leadership positions.

In no uncertain terms he made me aware of how upset he was, and he let others know too. However I couldn't satisfy him because I wouldn't reverse my decision. He subsequently distanced himself from me. Only brief, polite conversation was allowed. Any attempts I made to strengthen the relationship were thwarted. So what could I, should I, do?

This is one time that I responded to criticism in the right way. I prayed. Ken[14] was a good man with a heart for God. The Lord used him in special, sometimes remarkable, ways. He deeply loved the Word and sought the Lord with diligence. So I prayed for him, and the Lord changed my heart and renewed my love for him.

He and his wife usually sat in the sanctuary on the center aisle in the third or fourth row. So before service when I would see him there, I made it a point to walk past him, pat him on the shoulder and say, "I love you, Ken," and keep on walking. It drove him crazy! I confess that I'm so carnal that his discomfort gave me a great deal of self-satisfaction and pleasure!

After many months he came to me, and we made amends. We have been great friends to this day. But he said to me, "You know I've been upset with you. But no matter how ornery I was, you just kept loving me." I'm so glad I prayed for Ken, because prayer changed my attitude toward him.

Sometimes we may want God to change the attitude of our critics, but He wants to change us, and prayer is one of the tools He uses. When we sincerely pray for the person who has been our harshest critic, we

. . . .

Sometimes we may want God to change the attitude of our critics, but He wants to change us, and prayer is one of the tools He uses.

. . . .

can't stay angry at them. Any thought of revenge dissipates. Our hearts long to see them blessed.

Prayer Prevents Estrangement

When our attitudes are right, when prayer has filled our hearts with love, we can meet those who have been criticizing us with open arms.

Have you ever been in a war of words with someone? When you see them in the grocery store, you dart into the next aisle in order to avoid them. And what if you attend the same church? What effect does your estrangement have on the congregation? Most of the time, you can't tell that it makes any difference, but when two believers are at odds with each other it disrupts unity, creates dissension, and hinders agreement in prayer. But if we pray for one another, that has to change.

Reconciliation is always more precious than wrangling. Words that build up bear better fruit than words that tear down. Being able to look each other in the eye or give a hug is always more beneficial than avoiding one another. Fellowship is better than estrangement.

Prayer Fosters Forgiveness

Volumes have been written on the need for and value of forgiveness. I won't rehearse all those important lessons again. But we can all be reminded of Jesus' words, "When you stand praying, if you hold anything against anyone, forgive him, so that your Father in heaven may forgive you your sins" (Mark 11:25).

While we are praying, the Holy Spirit makes us aware if we are estranged from anyone because of unforgiveness. Sometimes I ask,

Holy Spirit, is there anyone I need to forgive? Do I harbor ill will toward anyone? Is my spirit rankled by unkind and thoughtless words someone said to me? The Holy Spirit is always faithful to answer those questions.

Prayer Guides Responses

We are learning that prayer should be our first response to criticism, but what about other reactions? Should we speak or be silent? Should we defend ourselves or let God be our Defender? Should we confront or ignore? Should we seek external counsel or rely only on our own discernment?

Answers to these and other questions can be clarified as we pray. Prayer has a way of sorting things out in our minds and hearts. We become more sensitive to the checks and promptings of the Spirit.

There have been times when I sensed the need to go and talk with the critic but to confront them would only aggravate the situation. So I've prayed, *Lord, give me a natural opening to talk with that person. Open a door of opportunity when I can discuss this matter in a non-confrontational way.* The Lord has answered that prayer many times, so that I've been able to respond in a way that brought healing to the relationship.

Remember—prayer is as much about listening as it is about talking.

Bless

As a minister I am in the blessing business. I have pronounced benedictions or blessings, not only at the conclusion of church services but at weddings, funerals, pastoral installations, ministers' ordinations, baby dedications, and more. So when Jesus says, "Bless and curse not," I have deep satisfaction knowing that I have said blessings over many.

The apostle Paul reiterates the blessing principle. "Bless those who persecute you; bless and do not curse" (Rom. 12:14). The word *bless* means "to speak well of." The Greek word for *bless* is the root from which the English word *eulogy* comes.[15] So when we bless someone, even a critic, we speak well of them. In other words, we do just the

. . . .

While in prayer we can ask for God's blessings on that person, even though they may have said falsehoods about us.

. . . .

opposite of what they have done to us. We don't stoop to their level in speaking harsh and unkind words, but we speak words of blessing.

Every person has good qualities that we can talk about. We should be quick to compliment that person for those qualities. "I appreciate your gift of hospitality." Letting others know about the positive aspects of that person's gifts will help to build them and others up. "Did you know that So-and-So is amazingly hospitable?"

Blessing and praying can be linked together. While in prayer we can ask for God's blessings on that person, even though they may have said falsehoods about us. "Lord, thank you for So-and-So. I pray that you will bless that person and their family. May everything they set their hand to prosper." We can pray biblical blessings over them, such as:

> The Lord bless you
> and keep you;
> the Lord make his face shine upon you
> and be gracious to you;
> the Lord turn his face toward you
> and give you peace.
> (Num. 6:24–26)

Where the pronoun *you* is used, insert the name of the person you are blessing.

When we are consistently praying blessing over those whose words have hurt us, it's extremely difficult, if not impossible, to continue to be angry with them.

Do Good

Doing good moves us from purely spiritual exercises to practical expressions of grace. They prompt us to take positive and proactive steps to build or rebuild relationships. We engage in these acts of love for several reasons.

1. Jesus told us to do it. "Do good to those who hate you" (Luke 6:27). Doing good reflects our obedience to our Master. Since it is already the pattern of our lives to do good, we don't stop doing good just because someone criticizes us.

2. Jesus modeled how to do it. "God anointed Jesus of Nazareth with the Holy Spirit and power, and . . . he went around doing good and healing all who were under the power of the devil, because God was with him" (Acts 10:38).

When describing the ministry of Jesus, the Bible is often the master of understatement. It passes over many of His good deeds lightly when in fact they were amazing works of power. For instance, at His arrest, Jesus healed the ear of Malchus, the high priest's servant. Peter had been flailing with his sword and cut the ear off. But in its understated way, the Scripture states, "Jesus . . . touched the man's ear and healed him" (Luke 22:51).

What an amazing act of grace! Malchus, armed like the mob with swords and clubs, was intent on arresting Jesus. Suddenly he found himself missing an ear. Can you imagine the pain! But so engrained in our Lord's character was doing good, He touched His enemy and healed him. Jesus is our model for doing good.

3. Beyond Jesus' words and example, the Bible encourages us to do good to our enemies. "For it is God's will that by doing good you should silence the ignorant talk of foolish men" (1 Peter 2:15). "If your enemy is hungry, feed him; if he is thirsty, give him something to drink . . . Do not be overcome by evil, but overcome evil with good" (Rom. 12:20–21).

4. In tangible ways, doing good shows the critic that from our side of things, hostilities are over and forgiveness has taken place. We are accustomed to hearing about random acts of kindness, but doing good is *not* random. It is intentional; it has purpose. It sends the message that we are at peace with the offender. Doing good is a peace offering to our enemies.

So bake their favorite pie and take it to them. Mow their lawn when they are on vacation. Send them flowers. Greet them with love when you see them. Speak well of them in their hearing. Send them a text, thanking them for a way they have blessed you. Sit near them in church so you can shake hands during the meet-and-greet time. Offer to help them with a difficult project. Shovel the snow from their sidewalk. Remember their birthday with a warm and happy card.

Pray for them. Bless them. Do good to them . . . and you'll discover that you truly love them.

Love

It's clear that Jesus' words—love, do good, bless, pray—are not a step-by-step formula ensuring perpetually happy relationships. We don't have to do one before another. I don't have to love before doing

- -

When people level criticism at us, it takes time to work through the emotions we feel.

- -

good. Doing good isn't a prerequisite to blessing or praying. They all work together, separately or simultaneously.

When people level criticism at us, it takes time to work through the emotions we feel. We may not be able to do immediately all that Jesus tells us we should do. We may have to do one thing at a time. Maybe we can begin by praying for the critic. Eventually that may lead to doing something good that sends an unmistakeable and positive message.

We begin where we can, but where we want to end up is—love. No matter what that person has said about us, regardless of how untrue or unjust their words may have been, in spite of the deep hurt they have inflicted, our goal is to love them without reservation. Tough assignment!

The truth is, we sometimes don't want to love them. We have no interest in developing any kind of relationship with them. We don't want to talk, work, or engage with them in any way. They can live in their orbit, and we will live in ours. But the Holy Spirit won't allow us to live that way. He will spur us to do what we don't want to do, but need to do. *Pray, bless, do good.* Actively pursuing these aspects of restoration leads us to genuine love.

That doesn't mean we should expect they will love us in return. They might, but they might not. They might persist in their criticism and be as cranky and quarrelsome as ever. But our hearts are secure in God's love, and in turn we are able to love them unreservedly.

Love, do good, bless, pray. That's the Jesus way.

Points to Ponder

1. While in prayer, ask the Holy Spirit if there is anyone you need to forgive. Then ask the Spirit to give you the power to do so.
2. Make a list of ways that you could do good to someone who has spoken against you. Then initiate action to implement one good deed. Ask for God's timing.
3. In your daily Scripture reading look for prayers and blessings you could adapt to bless one of your critics when you are praying for them. Examples are 1 Thessalonians 5:23–34; 2 Thessalonians 3:16; Hebrews 13:20; 3 John 2.
4. Develop a prayer list of people who rub you the wrong way. (Hopefully it won't be too long!) Each week, systematically pray through the list. Ask God to help you know how to pray and what to pray for.
5. Search your memory for someone who did good to you when you least deserved it. Thank God for that person.

o o o o

CHAPTER
7

Confronting the Critic

"I make my defense against all the accusations of the Jews."

Acts 26:2

"Spineless leader" is an oxymoron.—Dave Ramsey

Chris Christie, Republican governor of New Jersey, was giving a speech on the second anniversary of Superstorm Sandy. While he was speaking, a man in a pin-striped suit, holding a sign that read, "Finish the Job," began heckling him. His repeated and vehement interruptions expressed concerns that Christie had not moved quickly enough to release funds for the rebuilding of the Jersey Shore.

Finally Christie had enough and fired back. "I've been here when the cameras aren't here, buddy, and done the work. I'm glad you had your day to show off, but we're the ones who are here to actually do the work," Christie said. "So listen, you want to have the conversation later, I'm happy to have it, buddy. But until that time, sit down and shut up."[16]

Now that's one way to confront your critics! It's quite a contrast from "when we are slandered, we answer kindly" (1 Cor. 4:13).

Of course the political pundits pounced on Christie's outburst, speculating on his fitness to be a future presidential candidate. He was viewed as out-of-control, a hothead, and therefore disqualified for higher office. However, a reporter who covered him for four years disagreed. He made the point that Christie "controls almost every room, almost every situation—and almost always, himself. He can make crowds roar with laughter and go searching in their purses for tissues, all in the same speech. He can decide whether to yell back or ignore. Most of the time, I believe he knows exactly what he's doing when he does it. As Christie likes to say: 'I have more than one club in the bag.'"[17]

So maybe Christie's notorious bursts of anger aren't that at all. Some people interpret it as strength. They like his no-more-Mr.-Nice-Guy image. Whatever his motives may be, we are safe to say that Governor Christie doesn't respond the same way to every critic. Neither should we.

Scripture gives us this counsel: "Everyone should be quick to listen, slow to speak and slow to become angry" (James 1:19). The sequence is listen, speak, anger. The first is quick, the last two are slow. When criticized we're adept at reversing that order. Too often we are quick to anger, quick to speak, and slow to listen. "He who answers before listening—that is his folly and his shame" (Prov. 18:13). Dark memories of situations now past can conjure a bad case of the "If onlys." "If only I hadn't gotten angry. If only I hadn't said what I did. If only I had listened." But regrets don't turn back the clock. We aren't allowed any "do overs."

Anger is often the trigger that fires indignant, vocal bullets back at our critics.

A minister friend of mine was deeply invested in time, energy,

Angry words nearly always bear bad fruit.

and vision for a major church building renovation and expansion. The key moment for presentation and decision-making came at the annual business meeting. After laying the proposition out clearly and positively, he opened the floor for comments and questions. A major influencer took the microphone to question the proposal. After some sharp give-and-take, the pastor lost his temper and in front of the membership leveled the questioner and cut off discussion. His problem? He was quick to anger, quick to speak, and slow to listen.

The proposal was eventually accepted, but the pastor didn't see its fulfillment. A few months later he resigned. The respected influencer left the church. It was a sad ending to a scenario that didn't have to happen. Angry words nearly always bear bad fruit.

Proverbs offers these two contrasting, seemingly contradictory statements, one after the other: "Do not answer a fool according to his folly, or you will be like him yourself. Answer a fool according to his folly, or he will be wise in his own eyes" (26:4–5). So how are we to interpret this? Perhaps Solomon, the writer of these proverbs, is saying the same thing as James 1:19, but in a different way? There's a time to speak, and a time to be silent. These are key biblical principles to be applied when confronting a critic.

In previous chapters the emphasis has been on understanding the critic and formulating a spiritual response—heart issues, attitude, forgiveness. This chapter will focus on the strategy of responding verbally to criticism. There is a time to marshall a defense, particularly against unjust and untrue criticism. Chapter eight will deal more with the response of silence.

Who Is the Critic?

Our answers to criticism are conditioned by who said it.

Close relationship or not: When I wrote my first book I was startled by the number of people who disagreed with me on certain key points. While I took them seriously, I was under no constraint to answer all of them. Most of them were unknown to me. I had nothing invested in a relationship with them, so I had little to lose.

However, if close friends had shot such criticisms at me, which they were too kind to do, I would have been very careful in how I replied. I would have been careful not to say anything that would sever, or even damage, the relationship.

The closer the relationship, the more painful the criticism. Consequently, we must be careful about reacting to the pain rather than responding to the issues raised by criticism.

Christian or not: When the criticism is Christian vs. Christian, both understand and play by the same rules . . . or at least they should. The

Scriptures provide the playbook for how Christians ought to treat each other. But when the criticism is non-Christian vs. Christian, that changes things, because the non-Christian is playing by different rules. That person doesn't follow biblical guidelines.

In either case, we must follow the Scriptures. We can't risk sinking to the world's level in our attempts to resolve differences between ourselves and non-Christians. If they throw mud, we dare not get down in the mud with them. To do so will reduce any spiritual influence we might have on them. We may be tempted to think that a biblical approach will put us at a disadvantage, but in reality it gives us an unmistakeable edge. By overcoming evil with good, we'll always come out ahead. Even if we lose the criticism battle, we'll have won the spiritual war.

Criticism by those in authority over us is quite different from criticism initiated by those who are under our authority.

In authority or not: Criticism by those in authority over us is quite different from criticism initiated by those who are under our authority.

If my immediate superior at work pointedly criticizes my performance, I had better pay attention or I might soon be out of a job. I can defend myself by pointing out positive aspects of my work my superior missed, but this defense needs to be given with an attitude of submission. Mounting a major offensive against my boss will undoubtedly work against me.

When a leader is criticized by a follower, the challenges are stickier. For instance, if a cabinet member publicly criticizes the President, that member better have their resignation letter drafted and ready to turn in. Such criticism implies disloyalty toward the President, who requires a unified team.

In chapter two we looked at causes of criticism. Looking for such causes, the leader may ask, "Is it rebellion? Is it disloyalty? Is it frustration? Is it personal? Does it rise from insecurity?" If the motive behind the criticism can be discerned, then the leader will better know how to respond. This kind of scenario needs to be resolved between the leader and the follower and, if possible, behind closed doors.

Family or not: Family relationships present a completely different dynamic on the issue of criticism. The interwoven threads sewn together by moms and dads, siblings, aunts and uncles, cousins, and grandpas and grandmas are strong, resilient, and protective. I wish I could say that families are indestructible, but anger, harsh words, even violence have torn many families apart. The complexities of family criticism are beyond the scope of this book, but we've learned this about families: People can criticize their own families, but *you* better not criticize them! Even dysfunctional families can be tremendously loyal when attacked from the outside.

So when and how we respond to criticism can be determined in part by who is criticizing us.

How Did the Criticism Come?

Criticism isn't always packaged the same way, and its packaging may be the key to how we react or respond.

One to one: If someone must criticize, this is the best way to do it—privately and face-to-face. The criticism, and the damage it causes, is contained; it doesn't spread to others. This kind of meeting is far different than someone exploding while others are present. It minimizes anger. It provides for thoughtful, and perhaps prayerful, discussion. It can enhance relationships rather than destroy them. All of these positive outcomes are possible if the one criticized will respond with grace and love.

In public: If we're regularly in the public eye, we sometimes feel like the National Hockey League Hall of Fame goalie, Jacques Plante, who said, "How would you like a job where every time you made a mistake a big red light goes on and eighteen thousand people boo?"[18] For most of us public criticism isn't that bad!

However, some critics wait until you are *not* alone to take shots at you. They deliberately ambush you in front of other people. Their blasts come when you least expect it and are complicated by having others hear what is said. This becomes one of the biggest tests of the leader.

Others are watching how you answer and what spirit you manifest. When possible it's wise to defer a response. You can say, "I'm not prepared to answer you right now, but would be happy to meet with you later." That doesn't always satisfy the critic, but it shows a willingness to deal with the criticism without getting into a possible argument in front of those who have no "skin in the game."

In writing: We might immediately think that if we're criticized in writing, we should respond in writing. But in our social media culture, where Twitter, Facebook, texting, and emails are the primary means of communication, a reply in writing isn't always appropriate. Much depends on whether the criticism is public or private, i.e. Facebook or texting. Even when it is the latter, we need to exercise caution in writing a response for these reasons:

- What you have communicated in writing cannot be changed. When you put it in black and white, your words can't be taken back. Later we may wish we had said something in a different way, but once in writing it's too late to change.
- Written words can be read and referred to over and over again. Verbal communication can fade out over time. Written words never fade away.
- Words on paper usually come across stronger than what you would say if you were face-to-face. They are much more direct and forceful. One of my former staff members still teases me about a corrective memo I, the mild-mannered boss, wrote to all the staff that, as he put it, was still smoking when it arrived.
- Verbal communication is strengthened by the nonverbal—the look in the eye, the tone of the voice, the posture of the speaker, the attitude of the heart. None of these essential communication tools are available to the person reading a written response.

When I felt that a written response was needed, I would often pen a noncommittal letter, such as:

Dear Harry:
Thank you for your recent letter expressing concerns about (whatever the issue was). Like you, we have a desire for excellence

in all that we do. We receive your comments in the spirit that we are united, working toward the same goal of honoring our Lord in all we say or do.

May the Lord continue to bless you as you wholeheartedly serve Him.

Sincerely,
Pastor Warren

I suppose some might say that the letter is devious, but of course I don't think so. In the letter we:

- Send a response. We don't ignore the writer. Some people just want to know that you hear them.
- Express appreciation for the observations, but make no comment about their validity.
- Affirm the need for excellence which embraces the content of the criticism.
- Validate the desire for unity.
- Remind the critic that deeds and words must honor the Lord—a mild rebuke if the letter received was not Christ-honoring.
- Don't sever relationship or fellowship because of what was written.
- Maintain a positive and hopeful attitude.

Despite this bland letter, most of the time a written criticism will best be answered verbally. And remember, the best response to some criticism is no response at all.

When Is the Best Time to Respond?

The circumstances we have previously described are so varied that no single answer applies to the question of when to respond. Sometimes we must respond immediately. Other times we can defer . . . or we may not respond at all.

Don Ross, a leader of a large ministry network, speaks aptly to this issue: "I now wait to respond to a critical email, tough situation, or critical decision for at least three days. Time is an ally." He adds, "It seemed to me that waiting those three days somehow gave me the ability to recover my emotional and spiritual equilibrium."[19] It also gives us opportunity to think through what we might want to say or do. "Do you see a man who speaks in haste? There is more hope for a fool than for him" (Prov. 29:20).

What Is the Issue?

What issue has the criticism raised? What situation or circumstance set the critic off? Are others raising the same issue independent of the dominant critic? It's impossible to hit the target if you don't know which way to aim.

Personal or general: An attack on your personal integrity—"You're a liar"—is far different than a broad, general criticism—"I didn't like the Christmas pageant." The latter can be ignored, but the former cannot.

∙ ∙

It's difficult to separate criticism of something we do from criticism of who we are.

∙ ∙

The apostle Paul came under personal attack by the so-called "super-apostles" (2 Cor. 11:5, 12:11). They sought to undercut his work by denying his apostolic ministry. Paul was quick to defend himself against this unjust accusation. In fact, much of 2 Corinthians is given in defense of his apostleship. "The things that mark an apostle—signs, wonders and miracles—were done among you with great perseverance" (2 Cor. 12:12). Like Paul, we have every right to defend ourselves, correct the record, and rebut our critics.

It's difficult to separate criticism of something we do from criticism of who we are. Most of us are so invested in our work and ministries that any criticism in those areas seems to be directed at us personally. But often it's not. We need the wisdom of the Lord to discern the difference.

Attacks on our faith: Scripture encourages us "to contend for the faith that was once for all entrusted to the saints" (Jude 3). This is far different than dealing with personal criticism. Nevertheless the assault on our faith is reaching a crescendo.

Reports from Middle East war zones inform us of the wholesale slaughter of Christians because they won't deny their faith. Even children are being beheaded by ISIS (Islamic State of Iraq and Greater Syria) because they refuse to deny Jesus. The world is not worthy of these martyrs (Heb. 11:39).

In America, God is being systematically and deliberately driven from the public square, the market place, educational institutions, and the halls of justice. Christianity is marginalized, and Christ-followers are labeled as bigoted, intolerant, right-wing extremists.

In some ways, it's easier to respond to day-to-day personal criticisms than to this general societal trend that denigrates our faith. Each church and each individual must seek the Lord's guidance as to how to contend for the faith. Our intercessory prayers, our solid integrity, our consistent witness, our evident unity—all must serve as a prophetic voice to this generation.

Affirm the Person, Confront the Issue

In the book of Acts, Paul makes three lengthy defenses against the false charges others brought against him: (1) When mobbed by the Jews in Jerusalem and arrested (Acts 21–22); (2) at his trial before Felix (Acts 24); and (3) in presenting his case to Festus, Agrippa, and Bernice (Acts 26).

In the latter two cases he affirmed the person he was addressing. To Felix he said, "I know that for a number of years you have been a judge over this nation; so I gladly make my defense" (Acts 24:10). To Festus, Agrippa, and Bernice he said, "King Agrippa, I consider myself fortunate to stand before you today as I make my defense against all the accusations of the Jews, and especially so because you are well acquainted with all the Jewish customs and controversies. Therefore, I beg you to listen to me patiently" (Acts 26:2–3).

From Paul's example we learn that an answer couched in

graciousness at its beginning lays the groundwork for a clear defense. It separates the issue from the person we are talking with. Even corrective words are more palatable to the hearer when preceded by words of encouragement.

Nevertheless the issue must still be confronted. Doing so with grace lessens the tension surrounding the issue. I've found that asking questions to clarify the issue is helpful in some situations. Here are some starter questions and opening comments that I've used:

- **When you're unsure of the critic's motives:** Why do you say that?
- **When criticism seems to be ill-timed:** Why are you bringing that up now?
- **When emotions are running high:** I'm sorry that you feel that way. How can I help you?
- **When the issue seems to come out of left field:** Help me understand where you are coming from.
- **When the critic says "everyone" is unhappy or agrees with him:** Is this your concern alone or are you speaking for someone else? If so, who? This can't be resolved without knowing whom I should speak to besides you.
- **When confronted in public:** This isn't a good time to discuss this. I'd be happy to meet with you another time. What time would be convenient for you?
- **When you must remain noncommittal:** Thanks for bringing that to our attention.
- **When the issue is their problem, not yours:** Are you going to be able to get past this?

Strong leadership often requires that we mount a robust defense against criticism rooted in animosity and insecurity.

At the close of a face-to-face meeting, it's always helpful to conclude with prayer. This should be a prayer of blessing for the critic and that persons' family. Offering praise to God for that person lets them know that you have no animosity towards them. It's not uncommon for a critic to turn into a friend.

Strong leadership often requires that we mount a robust defense against criticism rooted in animosity and insecurity. In defending ourselves, we must guard our hearts against anger and words that wound. We may be in positions of leadership that would allow us to cut the critic down, but moral leadership is also required. We must model a Christ-like response to those who follow us. The critic may possess only a shriveled core of integrity. Our grace-filled response will reveal a level of integrity only made possible by our strong relationship with our Lord and Master.

Points to Ponder

1. Think back to your past reactions to criticism. Have you been slow to anger? Quick to listen? Slow to speak? What behavior patterns should you change with the Lord's help?
2. Is there one person who seems to be your nemesis? They seem to carp at you about everything. Think of one positive action you believe would strengthen the relationship . . . then do it.
3. Do you shy away from confrontation even when you know it's necessary? What holds you back? Fear? Anger? Frustration? Uncertainty about the reaction? Ask the Lord to help you overcome the obstacles that prevent you from confronting as you should.
4. Do you take every criticism personally, even when it is issue-oriented? Think of ways to change this pattern of behavior so you can separate the personal from the issue.
5. What steps might you take to enhance your listening skills? Take the first step.

o   o   o   o

CHAPTER

8

Divine Vindication

"Don't say, 'I will get even for this wrong.'
Wait for the Lord to handle the matter."
Proverbs 20:22, NLT

As leaders, there must be a point in our spiritual development where we can give God those who offend us, and let Him deal with the matter . . . in His timing.—Wayde Goodall

Most of Jesus' Sermon on the Mount is clear and understandable, but in my mind parts of it are still shrouded in mystery. I'm sure others have diagnosed and accurately interpreted every verse, but not me. While I value their learned exegeses, I'm not totally satisfied with them. In particular I'm stuck on the "eye for an eye" passage (Matt. 5:38–42).

Jesus' disciples, then and now, are challenged by His words. "You have heard that it was said, 'Eye for eye, and tooth for tooth.' But I tell you, Do not resist an evil person. If someone strikes you on the right cheek, turn to him the other also" (vv. 38–39).

Really?

If my enemies attack me physically, is my only recourse to allow them to continue to assault me? Christians are prone to joke about turning the other cheek by saying that Jesus didn't tell us what to do after the second blow—the idea being that we can then give our best punch! I don't think that's what Christ had in mind, so how are we to understand His words?

It gets even more complicated. "And if someone wants to sue you and take your tunic, let him have your cloak as well" (v. 40). So does this mean that if I'm sued, I can't defend myself? Or if the judge's verdict awards my opponent a large monetary judgment, am I supposed to give monies in addition to that judgment? How do Jesus' words work in the real world?

The Sermon goes on to say: "If someone forces you to go one mile, go with him two miles" (v. 41). Okay, that's a little clearer to me. If you are coerced into doing something, then be gracious and kind. Do more than is asked.

Finally, Jesus concluded this section of the Sermon by saying something even more outrageous. "Give to the one who asks you, and do not turn away from the one who wants to borrow from you" (v. 42). Oh, no! That can't be right, can it? *Jesus, surely you misspoke. Give to anyone who asks? Loan to anyone who wants to borrow? Isn't that dysfunctional stewardship? I can't believe you said that!*

But He did. All four statements came from Jesus, and no one was a clearer thinker or speaker about the kingdom than he was—after all, He is the King of the kingdom. So how are we to understand what He said? Did He mean for each of these four related thoughts to be taken literally, or are we to look at them through a different interpretive lens?

One of the recurring themes running through Matthew 5 is found in the words, "You have heard that it was said. . . ." Similar words are found six times in this chapter as our Lord contrasted the Law with the principles of the kingdom. He came preaching that the kingdom of heaven was at hand. Now He outlined what is sometimes called the Constitution or Magna Carta of the kingdom—the Sermon on the Mount. It's a study in contrasts. The Law was foundational, but now He wanted to introduce a new way of thinking and living. Like Jesus Himself, this kingdom-living is full of grace and truth.

The Law followed the eye-for-an-eye commandment. Avengers of blood weren't only allowed, but required. Vengeance was swift and immediate. But no more.

Think of the four directives we have cited above:

1. When struck, turn the other cheek.
2. When sued for your tunic, give up your cloak too.
3. When forced one mile, go two.
4. When asked to give or loan money, do it.

It seems to me that the new kingdom-principle Jesus introduced was this: *Followers of Christ do not respond to provocation in the same way as non-Christians.* Each of the four directives deals with provocation—physical attack, legal injustice, coercion, and pressured generosity. The non-Christian would respond to a physical assault in kind—an eye for an eye. To a lawsuit, there would be a counter suit. One mile would be more than a non-Christian would go. Give or loan? Not on your life.

Because of this principle I don't necessarily take Jesus' words literally any more than I take the admonition to gouge out an eye if it looks at a woman with lust (Matt. 5:27-29). The principle runs deeper than behavior. It rises from the heart. A heart changed by Jesus will respond far differently than an unchanged heart.

. . . .

Our response to criticism will be in sharp contrast to the way of the world.

. . . .

So it would follow that our response to criticism will be in sharp contrast to the way of the world. We have transformed hearts. Our attitudes differ from those around us. Even when mounting a justified defense, our spirits will reflect the Spirit within. Sometimes that same Spirit will prompt us to keep silent rather than to speak, pushing us into dependence on our Defender. "He who vindicates me is near" (Isa. 50:8).

Quiet Trust

Maintaining silence in the face of unjust, untrue, and damaging criticism is extremely hard to do. We are seldom "slow to speak." Rather we are quick to react and respond. Our retorts can be more caustic than the criticism that prompted them. But "in silence we consciously trust ourselves to God rather than following our human impulses to fix, control or put people in their place."[20]

When David was a fugitive, running for his life from King Saul, he had the opportunity to kill his royal pursuer. But instead he said to Saul, "May the LORD judge between you and me. And may the LORD avenge the wrongs you have done to me, but my hand will not touch you. As the old saying goes, 'From evildoers come evil deeds,' so my hand will not touch you" (1 Sam. 24:12–13). David trusted that the Lord would ultimately vindicate him, and his trust was rewarded.

Some of David's psalms are more easily understood in the context of the attacks from his enemies: "They have spoken against me with lying tongues. With words of hatred they surround me (Ps. 109:2–3). These imprecatory psalms, as they are called, were appeals to God to deal directly with those who had come against him. David's requests are specific, graphic, and seemingly judgmental.

But underneath the harsh words is a layer of spiritual understanding that knows God as One who can be trusted to right all wrongs. He is the final auditor of life's books and will ensure that they are balanced. His justice will impose righteous reprisals on David's enemies and will vindicate him. Of that David was confident.

Evident in young David's historic confrontation with Goliath are the seeds of a trust in God that would later ripen and mature. His "in your face" challenge to the giant reflects his total confidence in God: "You come against me with sword and spear and javelin, but I come against you in the name of the LORD Almighty, the God of the armies of Israel, whom you have defied. This day the LORD will hand you over to me, and I'll strike you down and cut off your head . . . for the battle is the LORD's, and he will give all of you into our hands" (1 Sam. 17:45–47).

David expected nothing less than full deliverance from the Philistine armies and their nine-foot-tall hero. David's quiet trust was in the Lord Almighty, also translated as Lord of Hosts.[21] The hosts/armies of heaven were at the disposal of the God Israel served. David had no doubt that the Almighty would act on his behalf, and that confidence brought Israel needed deliverance. David still whistled a stone from his sling at the giant's forehead, but the battle was the Lord's.

When we're in the thick of the battle, when harsh and hurtful

. . . .

When we're in the thick of the battle, when harsh and hurtful words are the weapons used against us, our trust remains in the Lord of Hosts, our Deliverer.

. . . .

words are the weapons used against us, our trust remains in the Lord of Hosts, our Deliverer. The hosts of heaven are at His disposal to defend and protect us.

Silent Strength

I heard a well-known pastor and author recount an experience from his years of pastoral counseling. One of the men in his church came to him for marital counseling. The conflict between this man and his wife was escalating, and he wanted the pastor's help. The pastor did what he could to encourage the man to deal with his part of the ongoing discord.

After a church service a few weeks later the pastor saw the man and asked, "Well, how are things going at home between you and your wife?"

The man replied, "Wonderful! I haven't spoken to her for two weeks!"

That was not the answer the pastor was expecting. He knew that it takes tremendous resolve and strength to give the silent treatment to someone you love. Where did such strength come from in this case? The pastor concluded that it came from anger. The angry words this husband had previously unleashed on his wife he now internalized with his silence. He was no less angry but simply expressed it another way.

This had devastating effects on the husband. Before long the pastor was called to visit the man in the hospital. The diagnosis? Bleeding ulcers. Anger made him strong enough to keep silent but damaged him physically. The source of his strength was negative, not positive.

So if we sense the Holy Spirit prompting us to be silent in the face of provocation, where does the strength come from to obey? Anger? Fear? Hatred? No, there are deeper reservoirs of strength to draw from.

I become alert to those deep sources of strength as I read and re-read the Gospel accounts of the trial and crucifixion of our Lord. As I do, I sense that I'm on holy ground. Here divine love is unveiled for all to see. Here salvation flows from sacrifice. Here silent strength is revealed.

Silence in the face of unjust accusation and criticism provides the world an opportunity to marvel at our strength and control.

As I read, I try to project myself back into Jesus' trial, to hear the cries, see the faces, and feel the raw emotion. In my mind's eye I can see the anger in the eyes and the sneer on the lips of those who cried, "Crucify him." I sense the hatred of the mockers, and listen to the blows of the hard-hearted soldiers. I hear the unjust charges brought against Him by false accusers. "But Jesus remained silent and gave no answer" (Mark 14:61).

Pilate, the politician, tried to pacify the mob, but they shouted him down, howling their lies and demanding the death penalty. Pilate acknowledged Jesus' innocence, but nevertheless ordered Him to be crucified. "But Jesus still made no reply" (Mark 15:5). In this maelstrom of chaos and violence, Jesus was the only person under control. Dripping with spit and blood, He was regal. He knew who He was and why He came—to be the Savior

"And Pilate was amazed" (Mark 15:5). Contrast Jesus' silence with the vehemence of the crowd. Contrast His strength with Pilate's weakness. Contrast His character with that of Barabbas. There is no comparison, and "Pilate marveled" (Mark 15:5, KJV).

Silence in the face of unjust accusation and criticism provides the world an opportunity to marvel at our strength and control. "To this you were called, because Christ suffered for you, leaving you an example, that you should follow in his steps. 'He committed no sin, and no deceit was found in his mouth.' When they hurled their insults at him, he did not retaliate; when he suffered, he made no threats" (1 Peter 2:21–23).

When we are quick to speak, responding with our own cutting and harsh words, we may believe we have overcome our critics. But the non-Christian will not be amazed or marvel. If we want that person to see Jesus in us, and thus marvel, then we must sometimes do what He did—be silent. We most often think of witnessing for Christ as something we say, and many times it is. But witnessing includes silence when Christ is revealed by what we don't say instead of what we do.

So where does the strength come from to keep silent? We could say that it comes from Jesus, or that the Holy Spirit gives us strength. That would all be true. But strength is not only something I receive. It develops from what I give. The key word here is *surrender.*

Before the trial and the crucifixion, Jesus went to Gethsemane. He reaffirmed His settled commitment to the mission of His Father. He surrendered. "Not what I will, but what you will" (Mark 14:36). His surrender was to the mission; He would do what the Father asked of Him. His surrender was to the suffering; He would bear unspeakable pain. But most of all, His surrender was to the Father. He would be obedient to all that the Father required.

Our surrender is not to our critics. It's to our Divine Vindicator.

"He entrusted himself to him who judges justly" (1 Peter 2:23). In other words, he surrendered Himself to the One who would bring ultimate vindication.

Knowing that his life was in God's hands, he could face anything, and so can we. He would speak when he should. He would be silent as well. He was confident that his vindication was assured because resurrection day was coming.

Our surrender is not to our critics. It's to our Divine Vindicator. Just as Jesus entrusted Himself to the Father, we do as well, knowing His vindication will be just.

Inner Dignity

Some of the sharpest criticism can be degrading, demeaning, and defamatory. It's intended to undermine our integrity, erode our self-confidence, and smear our reputations. It's motivated by the most negative of emotions—jealousy, fear, pride, and anger. When such criticism persists, we dare not give it any credence nor begin to believe it. Christ in us will help us maintain an inner spirit of dignity.

When critics resort to such damaging criticism, they reveal their true character. Their tactics are underhanded and deliberately injurious. But we must determine that we will not respond by utilizing the same tactics. We will not sink to their level, but will rise above it in our godly response.

Legendary radio preacher, C. M. Ward, told the story of a devout man named Henry Suso[22] who lived in a small German village. Such was his reputation that people from the region beat a path to his door to receive spiritual encouragement and wise counsel.

One day while standing on a street corner visiting with other men from the village, a young lady holding a baby rapidly approached them. When she reached Suso she vehemently thrust the baby into his arms and said, "Here, take the child of your lust!" Then she turned and ran away.

Suso stood there cradling the baby, inarticulate with shock and amazement. One by one the men with whom he had been visiting turned and walked away. Suso was left alone. He took the boy to his home and for twelve years cared for him as if he were his own. People no longer came to his home for prayer and spiritual direction. Yet not once during those years did Suso say a word in his own defense. He lived with dignity and grace, trusting his vindication to come from the Lord.

Finally after twelve years the mother returned. Her heart could no longer endure the separation from her son. She told the villagers that she had been as one possessed when she had last been in the village. She acknowledged that she had not known Henry Suso on that day long ago, except for his reputation for godliness, a reputation she purposed to destroy. Now she had come for her son, and they were reunited.

As word spread across Germany about this remarkable turn of events, Suso's integrity was lauded and his renown was further enhanced. In the face of the most severe provocation, he had surrendered his vindication to his God.

Whatever our response to criticism may be, and there are many, when we respond with the grace and dignity the Spirit gives, we can be confident of our ultimate vindication.

Points to Ponder

1. Read Matthew 5:28–32. Write down the ways these verses might apply to you. Is there a verse or a kingdom-principle that might apply to a present-day situation you are facing?
2. Think of a time when you were criticized but did not respond. Who or what gave you the strength to be silent?
3. When someone has thrown mud at you, and you have thrown mud back at them, how did you feel afterward? What could you have done differently?
4. Are there situations, issues, or people you need to surrender to the Lord? Through prayer release them to God.
5. Thank God that because of His surrender and sacrifice you can respond to criticism in a Christ-like manner.

o o o o

CHAPTER
9

Character Trumps Criticism

"It is God's will that your honorable lives should silence the ignorant people who make foolish accusations against you."
1 Peter 2:15, NLT

Remembering him [President Harry Truman] reminds people what a man in that office ought to be like. It's character, just character.
—Eric Sevareid

As I write this chapter, the National Football League is mired in a controversy that has been dubbed *Deflategate*. In the National Football Conference championship game, the Seattle Seahawks mounted a furious comeback in the closing minutes to tie the game, and then won 28–22 in overtime. What a finish! It was breathtaking—if you're a Seahawks fan.

But the American Football Conference championship game was a rout. The New England Patriots blasted the Indianapolis Colts 45–7. Frankly it was a boring game, but it moved the Patriots into the Super Bowl to meet the Hawks. However, things certainly got more interesting after the game.

An accusation was made that the Patriots had used footballs deflated below the required PSI (pounds per square inch). By rule the footballs are supposed to be inflated between 12.5 and 13.5 PSI. Upon examination, the league found that eleven out of twelve balls used by New England in the game were underinflated. Since the game was played on a cold, wet day, this deflation supposedly made the balls easier to throw and catch. The Colts used a different set of footballs, and so the assertion was made that they were at a competitive disadvantage. The outcome of the game wouldn't have changed even if everything had been on the up-and-up, but the possibility that one of the leagues' prime teams had cheated in a big game was headline news. Suddenly the issue wasn't only about football, but about character.

This incident resurrected a previous cheating scandal called Spygate, which also involved the Patriots. In 2007 they were caught illegally taping sideline defensive signals from the New York Jets coaches during the team's opening week game. At that time, accusations were leveled that this type of activity had been going on since 2000. The league penalized New England a first round draft pick and fined their coach, Bill Belichick, $500,000. So the question in the minds of many is whether or not cheating is part of the Patriots' culture. As one former football general manager put it, "Is there a culture of cheating at probably what most people look at as the best franchise in the National Football League?"[23]

Coach Belichick was quick to deny any knowledge of how or why the footballs were deflated. Those who know his penchant for control and attention to every detail were skeptical of his response.

The Patriots' quarterback, Tom Brady, held an extended press conference at which he responded to questions from the media. He also claimed to be ignorant of why the Patriots' footballs were deflated, but the Colts' footballs were not.

After watching the press conference, I listened to the responses of the sports commentators. The central question was, "Do you believe Tom Brady?" Many of the commentators—former football players—didn't think he was telling the truth. Hall of Famer Troy Aikman, who used to quarterback the Dallas Cowboys, when interviewed over radio said, "It's obvious that Tom Brady had something to do with this."[24]

However, other voices were raised in other venues regarding Brady's veracity. A common theme that ran through these comments, including those of former teammates and the Patriots' owner, was, "I've known Tom Brady for many years and believe him to be a man of integrity. I've never seen him cheat or try to gain an unfair advantage by going outside the rules. I respect him as a man of character." Brady's best defense throughout the Deflategate scandal was his reputation as a man of integrity. And in the aftermath of that scandal and its penalties, his best offense will be to live each new day as a man of integrity, before fans and critics both.

Although the official report did indicate that Brady 'probably' conspired to have the footballs deflated, the support he received and still receives from the people who know him best reminds us that a reputation for good character always pays positive benefits.

Occasionally I've had individuals speak derogatorily about a person I know well. They might point to a supposed misdeed, a lapse in judgment, or even some egregious behavior that violates biblical norms. My first response is to ask, "Is it true? How do you know? Is this just a rumor? What are the facts?" If it's based on hearsay, or blurbs from social media, or the rumor mill, it should not be believed or repeated. It's gossip. That tells you more about the talebearer than about the person being criticized. "A truthful witness gives honest testimony, but a false witness tells lies" (Prov. 12:17).

If indeed the accusation seems to be true, my second response is usually to say, "That doesn't sound like the person I know. The behavior you are describing is out of character with what I know of them." When you really know someone's character, that knowledge will trump criticism or charges against them, at least until proven otherwise.

Undivided

Integrity is the quality or state of being complete or undivided. So there's no division between our talk and our walk, between our lives at home and our lives at work or church, or between the private person and the public person. We're undivided. In other words, we're complete and consistent in our Christian walk.

That doesn't mean we're perfect or that we never make mistakes or sin against the Lord. David was a man after God's own heart, and his sin against God and Bathsheba had far-reaching ramifications for him and his family. But when you look at his lifetime of walking with

God, his essential character shines through his life and leadership. "And David shepherded them [*Israel*] with integrity of heart; with skillful hands he led them" (Ps. 78:72, emphasis mine). We do make mistakes, but people can sense when this is an aberration and not the pattern of our lives. But we must consistently walk the talk, living undivided lives.

. . . .

When we live and minister with an undivided heart, we have nothing to hide.

. . . .

Character and integrity are intertwined. If character is the tree, integrity is the fruit. If character is the skeleton, integrity is the flesh on the skeleton. If character is the heart, integrity is the life-blood. We can't have one without the other. We won't have one without the other.

Nothing to Hide

When we live and minister with an undivided heart, we have nothing to hide. No skeletons are hiding in the closet. The skeletons from our sinful past are under the blood. "There is now no condemnation for those who are in Christ Jesus" (Rom. 8:1).

The Enemy uses critics to bring accusation and condemnation. But when the channels between God and us are unobstructed, we can slough off the Accuser's false accusations. What others will see in our lives is authenticity and reality. Harboring hidden sins or misdeeds is not in our character.

"The man of integrity walks securely, but he who takes crooked paths will be found out" (Prov. 10:9). Make no mistake! If we walk on crooked paths, we cannot keep it hidden. It will come out. If today we have a divided heart, if we're not walking the talk, we need to confess our wrongdoing to the Lord. "He who conceals his sins does not prosper, but whoever confesses and renounces them finds mercy" (Prov. 28:13). Confession eliminates the skeletons, purges the spirit, and restores us to an undivided heart.

Nothing to Prove

A young minister friend of mine became the lead pastor of a well-known, very traditional church. He was an articulate speaker, an innovative thinker, and a gifted leader. He assembled a talented and energetic pastoral team. The church seemed poised to take a leap forward in its spiritual life and community influence. Alas, despite the best efforts of the pastor and his team, it was not to be.

His creative ideas for outreach into the city were met with a barrage of criticism. His weekly messages were assailed for encouraging change. According to some of his critics, he didn't give enough time to administrative detail. He was too nontraditional in his ministry philosophy.

Leaders at peace can become peacemakers, even with their critics.

But even his critics couldn't argue with the fact that he lived a godly life. He wasn't unaffected by the criticism, but he had nothing to prove. His life was consistent with his calling. He walked humbly before the Lord. He was like the man who fears the Lord, who the psalmist describes: "He will have no fear of bad news; his heart is steadfast, trusting in the LORD. His heart is secure; he will have no fear; in the end he will look in triumph on his foes" (Ps. 112:7–8).

After a pastoral tenure that was far too short, with nothing left to prove, he moved on with an undivided heart to a wildly successful pastorate. The critics were left to ponder the godly pastor they had just lost.

At Peace

Leaders of character, whose hearts are undivided, live at peace—peace with God, with themselves, and with others. They aren't easily puffed up by flattery, nor devastated by criticism. Their identity isn't found in what others say about them, good or bad. Their identity is in Christ. They affirm, "For to me, to live is Christ" (Phil. 1:21).

Leaders at peace can become peacemakers, even with their critics. God works on their behalf to blunt the sharp arrows of sarcasm and cynicism. Grace-filled responses can turn an enemy into a friend. "When a man's ways are pleasing to the LORD, he makes even his enemies live at peace with him" (Prov. 16:7).

Character vs. Competence

Bill Hybels, pastor at Willow Creek Church and prolific author, lists three areas he examines before hiring staff members: character, competence, and chemistry. I would add *calling* as a fourth important ingredient. Having good character doesn't ensure competence nor does it guarantee that the chemistry with other workers will be present. In ministry, one could have the first three, but without the calling and direction of the Lord, success isn't assured.

Criticism can be directed toward a person of good character who has an undivided heart because the individual is incompetent. The criticism is not leveled at an inconsistent life but at job performance. We can live sterling lives, but if we lack good wisdom in decision-making, we certainly will be criticized. If we don't possess sound judgment, if our people-skills are found wanting, if we are administrative disasters, or if our ability to communicate is impaired, our integrity and good character won't bail us out.

However, character is the foundation for effective leadership. Even if we are over the top in competence and chemistry, without character we will fail. But on the other hand, if our skill-set is wanting, a solid life of integrity by itself won't be sufficient for us to succeed. All the necessary elements must be in place. If they aren't, people will criticize us, and deservedly so. The criticism won't lessen until we shore up the areas of weakness in our leadership.

In Good Company

As much as we dislike being criticized, Jesus taught that one form of criticism and insult should cause us to rejoice! "Blessed are you when people insult you, persecute you and falsely say all kinds of evil against you *because of me.* Rejoice and be glad, because great is your reward in heaven, for in the same way they persecuted the prophets who were before you" (Matt. 5:11–12, emphasis mine). The emphasized words are the key: If we are insulted, persecuted, and maligned *because of Jesus*, we rejoice.

Luke's wording of the same teaching is even more descriptive: "Blessed are you when men hate you, when they exclude you and insult you and reject your name as evil, *because of the Son of Man.* Rejoice in that day and leap for joy, because great is your reward in heaven. For that is how their fathers treated the prophets" (Luke. 6:22–23, emphasis mine). Rejoice! Leap for joy! Your relationship with Jesus has marked you for special treatment—hatred, exclusion, insults, lies, persecution, and rejection . . . all because of Jesus. Knowing Him and serving Him is worth whatever price we must pay. We accept it all in Jesus' name.

The early apostles understood this mind-set. When they were brought before the Sanhedrin, they were flogged for preaching and ordered not to speak in the name of Jesus. "The apostles left the Sanhedrin, rejoicing because they had been counted worthy of suffering disgrace for the Name" (Acts 5:41). Did they stop preaching? Not a chance. "Day after day, in the temple courts and from house to house, they never stopped teaching and proclaiming the good news that Jesus is the Christ" (Acts 5:42). The message is always more important than the messenger.

. . . .

We dare not be intimidated by criticism aimed at Jesus in our lives.

. . . .

We dare not be intimidated by criticism aimed at Jesus in our lives. The good news is worth declaring whether the response is positive or negative. We can be, and sometimes should be, criticized for a multitude of issues that have nothing to do with our relationship with Jesus, and the Holy Spirit will give us clear direction as to how we should handle that criticism. But an outpouring of verbal abuse because of Jesus is not a cause for a stiff defense, but for a testimony of God's grace.

In Matthew 5 and Luke 6:22-23, Jesus reminds us that the prophets were also treated badly because of their obedience to their Master. So when we are criticized because of Jesus or because our character is becoming like His, we are in good company.

If we were to sift through our memory banks and remember the men and women of God from both the Old and New Testaments who were insulted, abused, and criticized for their relationship with God and the fulfillment of their calling, we could come up with a very long list. The Hall of Faith—Hebrews 11—lists many of them for us. Even today many Christians are giving their lives because of Jesus. So we can view criticism as a minor offense compared to those who are being martyred for their faith.

And think of Jesus, who was reviled, insulted, rejected, despised, and hated. Are we better than Him? No, we follow in His steps. "A student is not above his teacher, nor a servant above his master. . . . If the head of the house has been called Beelzebub, how much more the members of his household" (Matt. 10:24–25)! Persecution is inevitable for those who follow Jesus closely. So like the apostles we rejoice to be counted worthy to suffer for His name. We are in good company. And let's not forget the promise to those who suffer with Him, "Great is your reward in heaven."

From Grace to Grace

Our starting definition for grace was *"God's goodness to people who don't deserve it."* Is there anyone among us who deserves God's grace and goodness? No, what we deserve is hell and damnation. "We were by nature objects of wrath. But because of his great love for us, God, who is rich in mercy, made us alive with Christ even when we were dead in transgressions—it is by grace you have been saved" (Eph. 2:3–5). Because of grace we received what we didn't deserve—forgiveness, cleansing, salvation.

Receiving Grace

Even after the life-transformation experience of the new birth, grace continues to flow to us. In adversity and trial, and yes, even criticism, God's grace provides strength to deal with it.

Much has been written about Paul's thorn in the flesh. Despite the speculation of biblical commentators on the subject, the exact nature of that thorn is still unclear. However, Paul does make clear that it (1) was a messenger of Satan, (2) caused torment, and (3) was allowed to keep Paul from becoming conceited (2 Cor. 12:7). Three times Paul pleaded with the Lord to take the thorn away from him. Instead of answering Paul's prayer, God gave grace. "My grace is sufficient for you, for my power is made perfect in weakness" (2 Cor. 12:9). The weakness Paul experienced because of the thorn was the means by which God revealed the power of His grace.

Our stalwart individualism makes it difficult for us to acknowledge our weakness. We would rather quote, "I can do everything through him who gives me strength" (Phil. 4:13) than "I will boast all the more gladly about my weaknesses" (2 Cor. 12:9). When criticized, we may be convinced that we can handle our challenges without God's help. But in reality we need to receive grace and the power it provides. Grace *is* sufficient for whatever the critic, or messenger of Satan, may say about us.

So like Paul, we can affirm that "for Christ's sake, I delight in weaknesses, in insults, in hardships, in persecutions, in difficulties. For when I am weak, then I am strong" (2 Cor. 12:10).

Giving Grace

No matter how often we draw from the well of God's grace, there is always enough. Its supply cannot be exhausted. The well never runs dry. It provides enough, not only for us personally but for those who criticize and undercut us as well.

We may be quick to say, "They don't deserve grace!" True enough, but grace was specifically designed for the undeserving. And God's grace-supply to us is adequate also for them if we are willing to give it away.

Grace enables us to overlook verbal offenses and bury them in love.

Grace gives us the power to rise above self-pity, self-interest, and the giving-up spirit.

Grace empowers us to transform for our own benefit that which was intended to harm us.

Grace harnesses the unconquerable forces of loving, blessing, praying, and doing good.

Grace raises a stout defense while affirming the offender.

Grace rests in the assurance of God's vindication.

Grace develops the character that withstands verbal assault.

How do we cope with criticism? How do we deal with the inevitable—hurtful arrows shot at us? How do we keep criticism from derailing our leadership?

Grace! We've received grace from God, and now we give grace away to our critics.

Points to Ponder

1. What can we learn about character from Deflategate?
2. Prayerfully ponder your words and deeds. Identify any contradictions. What steps can you take for your walk and talk to be undivided?
3. Are you hiding certain bad behaviors from your spouse or best friends? Why do you keep them hidden? What would happen if you confessed them to God and others?
4. Evaluate whether your work ethic is consistent with your character. In what ways could you change your work/job so that you maximize your strengths?
5. Think of someone you admire because of that person's strong character. What character qualities do you admire most? Why?

o o o o

ENDNOTES

1. W. E. Vine, *An Expository Dictionary of New Testament Words* (Westwood, NJ: Fleming H. Revell Co., 1940), 3:307.

2. Ruth Haley Barton, *Strengthening the Soul of Your Leadership: Seeking God in the Crucible of Ministry* (Downers Grove, IL: IVP Books, 2008), 140.

3. Edwin Friedman, *A Failure of Nerve* (New York: Seabury, 2007), as quoted by Barton, 140.

4. E. Stanley Jones, *Victorious Living*, Dean Merrill, ed., (Minneapolis, MN: Summerside Press, 1936), 289.

5. *The Word for You Today* (Salem, OR: Peoples Church, 2013), February 17.

6. http://en.wikipedia.org/wiki/Naval_mine#Daisy-chained_mine.

7. Wictionary.org

8. Merrill F. Unger, "Elijah," *Unger's Bible Dictionary* (Chicago: Moody Press, 1957), 303.

9. Don Ross, *Turnaround Pastor: Pathways to Save, Revive and Build Your Church* (Mountlake Terrace, WA: Turnaround Church Coaching Network, 2013), 1.

10. W. E. Vine, *An Expository Dictionary of New Testament Words*, (Fleming H. Revell Co.: Westwood, NJ), 1:241.

11. Zayda Rivera, http://www.nydailynews.com. Sunday, December 8, 2013.

12. Anna Chan, "Carrie Underwood Praying for 'Sound of Music' Critics." www.today/popculture

13. Vine, 1:262.

14. The name has been changed.

15. Vine, 1:132.

16. Mollie Reilly, "Sandy Activist Whom Chris Christie Told to 'Shut Up' Says He's Not Backing Down," *The Huffington Post*, October 30, 2014, www.huffingtonpost.com·

17. Matt Katz, "Chris Christies' Greatest Weakness," www.politico.com, November 14, 2014.

18. Dave Ramsey, *EntreLeadership*. (New York: Howard Books, 2011), 239.

19. Ross, 29.

20. Barton, *Strengthening the Soul of Your Leadership*, 125.

21. The King James Version translates it as "LORD of Hosts." The Hebrew is *Yahweh* (LORD) Sabaoth (armies).

22. C. M. Ward was the voice of the Assemblies of God radio program *Revivaltime* for twenty-five years. The original source of the story he told is not known.

23. David Newton. "Ex-GM on Patriots' Culture of Cheating." ESPN.com.

24. David Newton. ESPN.com.

o o o o

ABOUT THE AUTHOR

Warren **Bullock has** served as a lead pastor in Oregon and Washington for nearly twenty-five years. He has provided leadership to the Northwest Ministry Network of the Assemblies of God and currently serves as the executive presbyter (Northwest Region) for the General Council. Bullock holds a ThB from Northwest University, an MA from Seattle Pacific University, and a DMin from California Graduate School of Theology.

Dr. Bullock has had a long association with his alma mater, Northwest University in Kirkland, Washington. He has served there as an adjunct faculty member, Alumni Association President, dean of the College of Ministry, and continues to serve on the Board of Directors. In addition he has served as chair of the Board of Advisors for the Assemblies of God Theological Seminary and is on the Evangel University Board.

Bullock travels widely as a speaker and consultant. He's an unofficial mentor to dozens of young pastors. He has authored numerous articles and the books *When the Spirit Speaks* and *Your Next Pastor*.

Presently he serves as a teaching pastor at Peoples Church in Salem, Oregon. He and his wife, Judi, live in Keizer, Oregon. They have two children and five grandchildren.

For More Information

○ ○

Foreword By Dr. Troy Jones, founder of Power2Grow Ministries and author of
From Survival to Significance

When Words Hurt
Helping Godly Leaders Respond Wisely to Criticism

Warren D. Bullock

For more information about these and other valuable resources visit
www.salubrisreources.com